EVIL MEN

EVIL MEN

MIRANDA TWISS

**with additional material by
SHELLEY KLEIN**

MICHAEL O'MARA BOOKS LIMITED

First published in Great Britain in 2003 by
Michael O'Mara Books Limited
9 Lion Yard
Tremadoc Road
London SW4 7NQ

Parts of this book first appeared in *The Most Evil Men and Women in History*,
published by Michael O'Mara Books Limited in 2002.

A CIP catalogue record for this book is available from the British Library

ISBN 1-84317-070-1

1 3 5 7 9 10 8 6 4 2

Designed and typeset by Design 23

Printed and bound in Great Britain by Cox & Wyman, Reading, Berks

CONTENTS

INTRODUCTION

The only unifying factor between the thirteen men who appear in these pages and the evil acts they committed is that they all wielded unlimited power over other people's lives. As a group, their own lives span sixteen centuries, from warmonger Attila the Hun in AD445 to the modern-day international terrorist Osama Bin Laden. Motivated by power, religious belief, political conviction, sadism, lust or driven by sheer insanity, the names of these thirteen men have become synonymous with evil throughout the world.

John Stuart Mill said that 'the dictum that truth always triumphs over persecution is one of the pleasant falsehoods which men repeat after one another till they pass into commonplace, but which experience refutes. History teems with instances of truth and goodness put down by persecution'. How many times have you heard someone say, 'What goes around comes around'? In the grand scheme of things we often choose to believe that human goodness will prevail, and that the evil-doers will get what's coming to them. But justice for the thirteen in this book is only occasionally meted out. Ivan the Terrible, Stalin, Pol Pot, Torquemada and Pizarro all died in old age and Idi Amin lives in comfort. Sadly, the most obvious lesson to be learnt from comparing the thirteen's heinous crimes is that they all show us just how very little we have learnt from our mistakes. The ability of people to 'see no evil, hear no evil' was just as prevalent during Saddam Hussein's reign of terror as it had been in Hitler's. Both were giving a large section of the population exactly what they wanted and, in exchange for this, some of the people chose to ignore the cruelties perpetrated on their fellow citizens while others were terrorized into silence.

Power draws people towards the centre from which it emanates. None of the people in this book have committed their acts of atrocity alone – all have had very willing and able accomplices. Whole sections of Cambodian, German, Russian, Ugandan and Iraqi society mobilized behind Pol Pot, Hitler,

Stalin, Amin and Saddam in conducting mass killings. When Ivan the Terrible created his army of henchmen, the *Oprichniki*, he had no shortage of volunteers. Attila's bloodthirsty army drew people from throughout the 'civilized' world and, for many Ugandans, Amin's promise of wealth and unlimited power over life and death led hundreds to join his State Research Bureau. Men and women followed these evil leaders because they knew that complicity was the path to influence, money and power. Despite having to deal with the unpredictability of their leaders, people followed their baser instincts.

It should be pointed out that many 'evil' reigns of horror were mercifully short. Pol Pot only attained supreme power for four years, Amin for eight. Stalin, on the other hand, remained in power for over thirty years and, when he died, there were mass outpourings of grief at the passing of 'Uncle Joe'. Despite the fact that he had been directly responsible for the destruction of millions of people's lives, he was revered for years after his death. Indeed, most of the evil men within these pages have their apologists who regard the reports of their atrocities as propaganda.

Of course, the portrayal of people as evil has its benefits. If your enemy is seen in a bad light, then any means to stop them becomes acceptable. Rasputin provided the perfect scapegoat with which to undermine the Russian Tsar and Tsarina. It was his power over them that was seen at the time as a malevolent force. He was corrupting the Tsarina with his licentious ways, and corrupting the Tsar by isolating him from his advisers. Rasputin was a vehicle through which to attack the worst excesses of the royal family and hasten the end of the monarchy in Russia.

Is evil ever justified? With two of the thirteen there is a point to be made in their favour. It is extremely doubtful whether Attila the Hun would have forged such a large empire if not for his infamy. Town after town fell to him without a fight, simply because the tales of his evil had preceded him. And Stalin took Russia from the wooden plough to a superpower in thirty years. He may have lost sight of the fact that human dignity and well-being lay at the heart of all progress, but would a nation so used to the absolute power of the Tsarist state have responded to a kindly leader?

We do not really understand evil – often taking it as an absolute rather than as a comparative word. Our concept of evil in the twenty-first century is dramatically different from previous centuries. Can you imagine attending a burning of heretics outside Westminster Abbey? It may seem a ridiculous concept, but thousands of ordinary people actively participated in and enjoyed such gruesome rituals.

In many cases, religion seems to have provided the thirteen with either a reason for inflicting their barbarity, or a tool for receiving forgiveness for their evil acts. If they felt that God was on their side, their enemies were not only against them but also against their God and therefore any acts committed could be justified. After each killing spree, Ivan the Terrible would spend weeks purging himself before the altar; Torquemada dressed in his monk's habit, and ordered the torture and executions of the supposed 'heretics'; Vlad the Impaler regularly attended church services, and Francisco Pizarro conquered and ravaged the Inca Empire in the name of Christ. God may represent love and forgiveness, but the history books are full of terrible deeds committed in the name of religion.

What makes evil so fascinating? Glancing through the pages of history, it is difficult to find any subject that has puzzled the intelligence of mankind more than the subject of evil. A book outlining the history of man's inhumanity to man is somehow more gripping than one detailing people's good deeds. Evil destroys the integrity, the happiness and the welfare of a 'normal' society, yet we are absorbed by it, maybe in the hope that we will learn from our mistakes, but more likely from a perverse desire to hear of others' misfortunes while we comfort ourselves with the thought that it could never happen to us.

MIRANDA TWISS

ATTILA THE HUN

THE 'STORM
FROM THE EAST'

*A man born to shake the races of the world. The proud man's
power was to be seen in the very movements of his body.*

PRISCUS OF PANIUM

In the fifth century, one man brought terror and destruction to
millions. Attila the Hun led thousands of bloodthirsty
barbarians across the plains of Europe, bringing torture, rape,
and death to all who stood in his way. He acquired a vast
empire that stretched across parts of Germany, Russia, Poland
and much of south-east Europe. Known as the 'Scourge of
God', he struck fear into the mighty Roman Empire with his
savage methods of brutal destruction, razing cities to the
ground and killing thousands in his pursuit of gold and power.
Legend has it that the Huns dipped their arrows in the juice of
boiled embryos, drank women's blood and were descended
from the unclean spirits of the wilderness.

Mass slaughter, rape and pillage had been an integral part
of life for most of Northern Europe for centuries. Though the
Greeks and Romans had established the Mediterranean as the
cradle of civilization, it was constantly rocked by murderous
incursions from barbarian hordes to the north. Greek historian
Herodotus described savage Scythians who skinned opponents
to make coats, sawed off the top of their skulls to make
drinking cups, and drank the blood of their victims. Wild
Goths swept south from Sweden, and in AD410 sacked Rome in
a six-day orgy of rape and killing. Vicious Vandals reached the
city less than fifty years later, after storming through Germany,
Gaul, Spain and North Africa, leaving death and destruction in
their wake. Saxons, Franks and Vikings were other warlike and
unmerciful raiders. But of all the brutal barbarians who
terrorized Europe, none struck greater fear into men's hearts

than that of the Huns; they rode as fast as the wind, and were as bloodthirsty as wolves.

The Huns first invaded Europe in the fourth century, descending from the borders of China. In the early centuries of the Christian era, a widespread movement of people was taking place throughout northern Europe. The climate was undergoing drastic changes, ensuring long winters and very short summers. The Huns, who lived a plain, hard existence in an area stretching from Siberia to Korea, found they were unable to sustain themselves in the everlasting winter that descended.

Few accounts of their day-to-day lives exist – they did not keep written records, but what is known, however, is that they were well used to migrating, taking everything they owned, including the yurts (tented houses), which were designed for mobility.

After a period of plundering the fertile Yellow River in China, the long migration began; an entire nation headed west and south for thousands of miles. Some invaded Persia and Asia Minor, but the majority moved through Russia toward Europe where native tribes were overrun. In their travels toward the Roman Empire, the Huns were confronted by a variety of peoples, with many of whom they did battle. Some people were more willing than others to accept the kind of dominion the Huns imposed. Some swelled the flood of refugees, and others provided valuable additional manpower to swell the ranks of the Hun armies. Finally, the vast exodus settled on the Hungarian plains, north of the river Danube, between the Volga and Don. The Roman Empire, on whose borders they now lived, initially fought them for a few years, and, from the year AD410, chose to establish an uneasy détente with the Hun King, Ruga.

Unlike the earlier Roman Republic, the Roman Empire was not an aggressive, expansionist state. Its frontiers in Europe ran for over 2,000 kilometres. Frontier defence was not, for the most part, required; there were no threats from other major powers. For centuries, the only kingdom that the Romans had had any need to fear, or to respect militarily, was the Persian Empire of the Sassanids. However, all that would change with the coming of Attila.

Born in AD406, Attila lost his father when he was very young. Like all Hun males, Attila was encouraged to ride before he could walk, and fight – using bow and arrow – by his fifth birthday. Brought up in a deeply superstitious society, amongst people who surrounded their camps with horses heads on sticks to ward off evil spirits, Attila became well attuned to listening to prophecies, a trait that remained with him throughout his life, and served him well.

At the beginning of the fifth century, Rome bought peace for itself from King Ruga, Attila's uncle. They paid an annual tribute of 350 pounds of gold, and both sides took high-ranking hostages as a guarantee of good behaviour. Thus, Attila was exchanged with a young nobleman, Aetius, and sent to live in Ravenna, in the Western Roman Empire. Here, Attila learnt to speak, read and write Latin. He admired the Romans' strict organization, but quickly came to despise their decadent tendencies. In fact, Attila was witnessing the final glory days of the Empire, before its own decadence and corruption destroyed it, and these learning years would one day make him Rome's most dangerous enemy.

In his early twenties, Attila returned to his people. He was involved in several murderous Hun invasions, spurred on by King Ruga, who believed that 'everything the sun shines upon I can conquer'. However, when Attila was twenty-seven, King Ruga died and was succeeded by Attila's brother, Bleda. Attila was said to be furious, but he initially hid his frustration and carried on building his reputation as a lethally effective military leader.

By now, Attila was a striking figure, with a large head, swarthy complexion, small, deep-seated eyes, a flat nose and a few hairs in place of a beard. He had broad shoulders and a short, square body. Early on, he had realized the power of a ruthless image, and allowed his men freedom to inflict the worst possible atrocities on their enemies. He purposefully created an army of bloodthirsty sadists.

To the civilized Romans, the Huns were savages: they ate

raw meat, lived and slept on horseback, didn't wash and were known to be untrustworthy. The Huns were also expert horsemen and known for their lightning attacks – the medieval equivalent of the twentieth-century blitzkrieg. Surprise and terror were of the essence. The first sign to alert a settlement to a Hun raid would be a cloud of dust, followed by the sky turning black under a hail of arrows, before the Horsemen of the Apocalypse unleashed hell. They could fire arrows forwards, backwards and sideways, while standing on horseback, and could kill a man at 150 metres. While other empires only had bows that could draw a few centimetres, the Huns had developed ones that could draw up to thirty.

The secret behind the Huns' strength was an almost modern infrastructure. News could easily be relayed to far-away dominions by carriers who rode over thousands of miles, to deliver messages to every corner of the Hun world. Using reserve horses, they could ensure that no other message travelled as fast as theirs did. Many of the conquered people also became slaves of the Huns, and when Hun nobles went to war, their retinues would consist equally of slaves and free men.

It wasn't surprising therefore that, after King Ruga's death (an event initially regarded by the Roman Empire as an excuse for suspending any agreements with the Huns), emissaries from Constantinople, cowed by the might of the Hun forces, signed the Treaty of Margus in AD435 and agreed to double their annual tribute to 700 pounds of gold. They also agreed not to enter into any alliances with enemies of the Huns, and to return all Hun prisoners.

For the Huns, the treaty was an unqualified triumph, and Bleda and Attila directed their attention away from the Balkans and started to consolidate their empire in the direction of the Alps and the Rhine. But in AD439, a series of wars against the Roman Empire broke out on a number of fronts. Bleda and Attila now realized they could resume their plundering of the Balkans and, obtaining gold from the Bishop of Margus, who knew the Huns were not going to be deflected, they swept onwards.

In his late thirties, Attila attacked and decimated the city of

Naissus; in fact, the riverbanks became so littered with human bones that for years after no one would enter the city because of the stench of death. Attila enjoyed the apocalyptic scenes his men caused. He had a habit of fiercely rolling his eyes, in order to inspire greater terror in his victims.

But a man of Attila's commanding and ruthless personality did not relish remaining second-in-command indefinitely, and in AD445, frustrated at his lack of power, he murdered his brother, Bleda, in cold blood, and took the throne.

Becoming king in his early forties had given Attila time to plan his reign of terror. As a ruler, Attila was an originator, and in some respects a revolutionary. He knew that if the Huns were to be a great power, as he intended them to be, they must learn from other, more advanced, peoples. He was wary of creating a threat within Hunnick society, and discouraged literacy amongst his people, seeing the danger of having subjects with too much education and ambition. In consequence, his own intimate circle of advisers consisted largely of foreigners, and he purchased many of their services with gold. It has been suggested that one reason why Attila surrounded himself with foreigners is that, after Bleda's death, he no longer trusted prominent Huns. One of Attila's advisers, Orestes, was married to the daughter of the military commander of a Roman province. Bringing his wife with him, he came to the Hun court to offer his services. Attila's principal secretary, Constantius, came from Italy.

But Attila needed ever-increasing amounts of gold – the Hun Empire's main profession had been war and, plunder and, with every territorial gain, further demands were made on Attila to provide for his new subjects. He also needed to consolidate his authority over the large number of tribes within the expanding Hun Empire. With this in mind, Attila, realizing the power of collaboration, galvanized not only the Hunnick tribes, but also the various barbarian groups – such as the Visigoths, Gepids and Vandals. United, they were a significant force – Attila now had up to half a million savage warriors at his disposal, enough fighting power to defeat an empire. When an ancient sword was found by one of his tribesman, it was believed to be the sacred sword of Mars. Attila now believed he was invincible and that it was his destiny to lead his people to ultimate victory. Like crows snatching prey from an eagle, the Huns now threatened the Roman Empire.

The Roman Empire was divided into two halves – Eastern and Western Empires. Attila first set his sights on the East, which contained the largest city in the world, Constantinople (a city we know today as Istanbul). He instructed his forces to actively destroy the lands they conquered between the Black Sea and the Mediterranean, to heighten fear and suppress resistance.

The Huns pillaged churches and monasteries, slew monks and virgins, and desecrated the graves of saints. Attila captured more than a hundred cities and the death toll was so high that no one could even count the dead.

However, Attila's ultimate objective was the capture of Constantinople, and his campaign was thus conducted with a thoroughness not shown previously by Hun armies, although, from time to time, detours were made so that additional cities could also be captured and destroyed. One such was Sofia, on whose ruins a Slav people would later build a new city.

By March AD447, Attila's forces were approaching Constantinople; the citizens were in a blind panic at the imminent arrival of the Hun armies, and thousands fled. Attila, however, failed to launch an attack, because his army was incapable of using the siege techniques necessary to subdue a city as substantial and as well defended as Constantinople. His troops were also riddled with disease, principally malaria and dysentery.

But the army was only halted by sickness, it was not overcome, and Attila remained a perpetual menace to the well-being and security of Constantinople and, indeed, to the whole of the Eastern Empire. Knowing this, he continually increased his demands. The annual tribute already stood at 6,000 pounds of gold and Attila sent one emissary after another, calling for new exactions. However, the war had seriously diminished the Eastern Roman Empire's treasury; vast amounts of precious metals were melted down to meet Attila's demands.

Attila also repeated, more implacable than ever, that all Hun prisoners should be released and, in addition to this, he insisted on the handing over of men of any race who had transferred their loyalty from the Huns to the Empire. Many men chose death at the hands of imperial officers rather than return to the dreaded Huns. The prestige of the imperial army, unable to protect its own recruits, plummeted disastrously.

Every pound of gold that crossed the Danube made Attila more powerful and intimidating, and further humiliated the Romans. He had created so much devastation and fear that he was unopposed in the Eastern Roman Empire. Now he could plan his attack on the West. Finally, it all became too much for the Romans, and a plot was hatched to murder Attila. One of his allies, Edika, the Skirian king, offered to kill him for 50 pounds of gold, but Attila discovered the plot and dealt with its perpetrators.

Attila, although now king of a vast empire and millions of subjects, still kept his barbaric ways. Though he would entertain foreign dignitaries, serving them the finest food on silver plates and wine from golden goblets, he would only eat a lump of raw meat served on a wooden platter, and drink wine from a wooden goblet. Rumours of his cannibalistic practices are not unfounded; he is believed to have eaten his own sons, Erp and Eitil, after his wife served them to him roasted in honey. The Hunnick practice of polygamy was also well suited to Attila's tastes. He is said to have fathered over a hundred children, with a vast number of wives.

In AD450 Theodosius II, Emperor of Eastern Rome, died and was replaced by Marcian. Theodosius's death deprived the Western Roman Emperor, Valentinian III, of one of his most experienced statesmen. The Roman Empire was not the force it once was, with incursions becoming a regular occurrence, and generations of complacency leading to political infighting. Then, in AD450, Attila received an extraordinary offer.

Honoria was the sister of the Emperor of Valentinian III, but she had become an embarrassment and had been banished to Constantinople, after being caught having an affair with her chamberlain. Desperate to escape a regime of prayer and fasting, Honoria, entrusting a eunuch called Hyacinth, arranged to smuggle her gold ring to Attila as a proposal of marriage. Her mother had been married to a barbarian king, and she saw the advantage of a union between the powerful leader of the Huns and the sister of the Roman Emperor. Attila saw the benefits of the collaboration, too. He was already plentifully supplied with wives, but Honoria's advances fitted his own plans in a way he could hardly have hoped for. He accepted her proposal of marriage, adding, with splendid panache, that the dowry he expected to go with it was half the Western Roman Empire.

The Emperor Valentinian denounced his sister's actions and turned down Attila's demands. Attila declared war. With the excuse he needed, Attila unleashed the might of his combined barbarian armies into western Europe. In AD451 the Huns left their settlements in Hungary, and Attila's vast army crossed the Rhine through Germany and towards France. Attila claimed he was merely reclaiming his rightful lands, but this was simply an excuse to gain more riches.

His army of between 300,000 and 700,000 was the largest that Europe had seen since the expansion of the Roman Empire, over two hundred years before. They were intent on wreaking havoc on a large scale, and did precisely that. Many of Europe's great cities were conquered, including Rheims, Strasbourg, Trier and Cologne.

While passing through Germany, Attila encountered St Ursula, the perpetual virgin. Attila was smitten and – putting his mission for Honoria to one side – proposed marriage to the chaste pilgrim. When she refused, he killed her with an arrow and slaughtered 11,000 of her pilgrim companions.

Attila's army tore into France, destroying everything in its path. When the warriors entered Metz just before Easter, they 'gave the city to flames, and slew the people with the edge of the sword, and did to death the priests of the Lord before the holy altars.' The destruction at Metz was a foretaste of much that was to occur as Attila's army advanced through France. City after city, we learn from the Christian chroniclers, suffered destruction as a punishment for the sins of the people. Where destruction and death were avoided, it was put down to divine response to the supplications and conduct of the pious. Nowhere, however, is it suggested that Attila's armies conquered through superior military skills.

Attila was a deeply superstitious man, who paid close attention to the pronouncements of his priests, soothsayers and shamans, and he allowed them to influence military decisions. As Attila approached Paris, he had a premonition that to attack the city would bring bad luck. Other cities would not be so lucky. But the tide was about to turn.

By May AD451, Attila's army had reached Orleans. Here, they encountered heavy resistance. Orleans had been garrisoned by the now famous Roman commander, Aetius, who had spent his childhood with the Huns, and the city remained a fortress, however much Attila battered at its doors with his army. The city was saved by the arrival of Roman legions, allied to an army of Visigoths.

The successful resistance of the city of Orleans was an unpleasant and disturbing experience for Attila. In his campaigns in the Balkans and throughout Germany and France, he had become accustomed to cities that surrendered to him or which could be destroyed at his will. Only Constantinople, with its virtually impregnable walls, had been unattainable. Attila withdrew to the plains near Châlons-sur-Marne and prepared for battle.

The Battle of Châlons, or the Catalaunian Fields, became notorious for its brutality. The hand-to-hand fighting was so fierce that rivers of blood were formed and those thirsty from the fight had to drink water mingled with gore.

Attila was up against a formidable opponent – Aetius – a man who knew as much about the Hun mentality as Attila knew about the Romans. Aetius had arrived in France after a long trek over the Alps and had accumulated vast numbers of allies to fight by his side.

On the day battle commenced, Attila stood on the vast, flat plain surrounded by his army, with leaders of each tribe hanging upon his command like slaves. 'When he gave a sign, or even a glance, they obeyed him without a murmur.' His army then began discharging a large number of iron-tipped arrows, guaranteed to penetrate leather battledresses, and a cavalry engagement followed. Attila and his allies gained an initial advantage by breaking through in the centre, after which they turned their attention to the Visigoths, who drove Attila back behind their defences. So it was that victory, although not decisive by any means, had gone to the armies of Rome and its allies.

Attila decided he must prepare for the worst. This was not death, but capture, and he had his own funeral pyre prepared. Wooden saddles and other cavalry accoutrements were piled up, ready to be set ablaze if necessary. But all was not going well, either, for the Roman commander, Aetius. The Visigoths, under Thorismund's command, abandoned the Romans on the battlefield. Aetius knew that without their support, he would be in serious danger of defeat.

Attila, meanwhile, was astonished that Aetius had failed to exploit the advantage he had gained, and that the fighting had suddenly stopped. At first, he believed that the sudden retreat of the Goths was a stratagem intended to lure him into an injudicious attack, so he remained immobilized for some time, in the defensive position he had taken up. Then, when no action followed, he began to withdraw. Like Aetius, he could not be certain of victory.

The Battle of Châlons has been described as one of the fifteen most decisive battles in history. Had the Romans not won, Europeans today would be the direct line of descent from Attila and his Mongol hordes.

Further atrocities were committed by Attila's army. In retreat, they massacred their hostages as well as their captives; 200 young maidens were tortured with exquisite and unrelenting rage – their bodies were torn asunder by wild horses, or their bones were crushed under the weight of rolling wagons, and their unburied limbs were abandoned on the public roads as prey to dogs.

Attila's campaign in France had been a disappointment to him. He had lost large areas of territory and was returning with considerably less booty than expected. Almost immediately after his return to Hungary, he was making further demands for large quantities of gold, and doing so without being in a position to back his demands with adequate force.

Theodosius's successor, Marcian, now began to exhibit both strength and statesmanship. He had refrained from attacking Attila's kingdom while he was away in France and Germany, but he had no intention of giving Attila any more gold.

Almost before his army's battle wounds had healed, Attila gave orders for them to fight again. Despite their arduous return to Hungary over the Alps, the Huns were still eager. War was their industry, and Attila's reputation had been largely unaffected by the defeat at Châlons.

Once again, Attila had asked for the hand of Honoria, the Emperor's sister, and had been refused. This time, he decided to take his demands straight to Rome. Attila believed that to invade Italy was a logical consequence of demanding half of the Western Empire as Honoria's dowry. He also knew that if he was going to achieve his ambition of conquering the world, then Rome would have to fall.

Attila set off for northern Italy in the spring of AD452, once again commanding an international force of Gepids, Ostrogoths, Skirians, Swabians and Alemens. Because of the absence of the Hun forces in Armenia, it was certainly more Germanic than Hun in composition. The army moved towards Trieste, but was halted at Aquileia, a fortified town of major importance. Whoever held Aquileia was likely to command much of northern Italy. Attila decided to lay siege to the city, but at the end of three months, there was no indication that the garrison was considering either surrender or abandonment. Attila was on the verge of giving up the siege; however, legend tells us that, just as he was making the preparations to retreat, a single white stork rose from a tower on the city wall and, with his young upon his back, flew off away from the city. When the superstitious Attila saw this, he commanded the army to remain. Shortly afterwards, the section of wall containing the abandoned tower fell down, and Attila was able to storm the city.

The destruction inflicted upon Aquileia was total, and it never again became a city of importance. The news of what had happened spread like wildfire throughout Italy, and the rulers of other cities took note. From Aquileia, Attila's army then moved to Padua. This was a major city, supported by thriving agriculture and industry, with large numbers of important citizens. Attila's forces plundered it thoroughly, but before his arrival, a large number of people fled into the swamps, knowing that Attila's largely horse-driven army could not follow. The city they were to found was Venice.

As Attila's army advanced through Italy, they no doubt felt deeply content. Not only were they unopposed by any hostile army, but they increasingly found that the gates of the cities were opened to let them in. They were not so much made welcome, as recognized to be a force that it would be unwise to resist. The way was open to the former imperial capital, Milan.

Valentinian now fled from his temporary home in Ravenna to Rome, still hoping to find some effective means of resisting Attila's hordes. Meanwhile, Attila captured Milan, briefly occupying the royal palace. Here, he was reported to have asserted his power over Rome in a unique manner. A painting in which Caesars were depicted sitting on thrones, with Sythian princes prostrate at their feet, caught his eye and he ordered it to be changed. Now the Caesars were shown as suppliants, emptying bags of gold before the throne of Attila himself.

After Milan, Attila led his men deeper and deeper into Italy. The Horsemen of the Apocalypse had arrived – people fled in panic, but they had few places to hide. By the time he reached the River Po, Attila's army was having to deal with a new enemy – malaria – which was ravaging his troops. But luck was on his side, and once more, the terror that his name inspired had done its work for him. The Emperor Valentinian was truly intimidated; fearing an empire would be lost, he sent a delegation to appeal for a truce. Attila agreed to negotiations.

On the River Mincio he was confronted by Pope Leo I and two advisers: Trigetius, the Prefect of Rome and Gennadius Avienus, a rich and successful politician. Their job was to persuade Attila not to attack Rome. Attila received them, lying in his tent. He was certainly not overawed by them; they were the supplicants, not he. The contemporary historian, Priscus, relates that 'Attila's mind had been bent on going to Rome. But his followers took him away and reminded him that the last person to conquer Rome, Alaric the Visigoth, had not lived long after the event.' Attila's priests foretold disaster if he continued and so, faced with his disease-ravaged troops, polluted water, chronic heat and a shortage of food, he sensibly decided not to enter Rome. Instead, Attila and his barbarian hordes left, loaded down with great treasures, and headed home to the Hungarian plains.

Within a few months, Attila seemed to regret the peace and was vexed at the cessation of war. He sent ambassadors to Marcian, threatening to devastate the provinces because of what had been promised to him by Theodosius, saying that he would show himself crueler to his foes than ever. Such threats were never realized, however, as his reign of terror was soon to end.

By AD453 Attila was in his fifties. Despite his grand age, he retained his voracious sexual appetite. On 15 March AD453, he married a young, beautiful German noblewoman, Ildrico. Legend has it that she had vowed to make Attila pay for the murder of so many of her countrymen. What is known is that after a wedding of great feasting and drinking, Attila retired to bed. By the morning, he was dead – an artery had burst and Attila had drowned in his own blood.

With his death, the now leaderless empire broke up. The Huns had ravaged Europe for almost two centuries. His men cut off their hair and disfigured their faces with deep scars so that Attila, their glorious hero, would be mourned, not by the tears of women but by the blood of men.

His body was laid in state, and his saddle and clothes burnt. Horsemen from the entire Hun population circled around, and a dirge was sung for one of history's most savage warriors. During the night, the body was secretly put into the earth. Within a year, the only two leaders who had successfully defied Attila, Aetius and Thorismund, were also dead.

A large number of the Huns who were scattered over half of Europe went back to the Mongolian steppes. By AD476 the

Western Roman Empire came to an end, with the abdication of Romulus.

Attila the Hun had ruled for only eight years, but the terror that he brought to the population of fifth-century Europe ensured his name is still synonymous with death and destruction to this day. Legends in which Attila was the central figure began to take shape soon after his death. Different countries and their legends have chosen to portray Attila in a variety of guises; some underplay his brutality, while others revel in it.

TORQUEMADA

THE SPANISH INQUISITOR

I hold you in the very bowels of affection for your immense labours in the exhalation of the Catholic faith.

POPE ALEXANDER VI

'In view of the suspicions arising against him from the evidence, he is condemned to be tortured for such a length of time as should be seen fit, in order that he might tell the truth. If in the torture he should die or suffer effusion of blood or mutilation, it should not be attributed to the Inquisitors, but to him for not telling the truth.'

As head of the Spanish Inquisition, Tomás de Torquemada was responsible for the imprisonment, torture and death of thousands of innocent Spaniards. Known as the 'Black Legend', he spread fear throughout the land, wielding a power and an influence rivalling the monarchy of King Ferdinand and Queen Isabella. He developed his institution with pitiless zeal and ruthless fanaticism. Clad in the austere garb of a Dominican friar, the gaunt, sunken-eyed sadist vented his hatred on Jews and heretics, forcing up to 300,000 out of Spain and destroying their lives forever.

The idea that religious dissent should be punished by force is almost as old as Christianity itself. In the year AD385, the pious Emperor Maximus had tortured and executed the heretic Priscillian and some of his followers. In the Dark Ages the persecution of heretics seems to have fallen into disuse, but during the Middle Ages it was finally revived and elaborated on. The Catholic Church faced a crisis from the Albigensian religious movement in the South of France. The Pope therefore sent troops to eradicate the heretics, but soon realized that they had not been obliterated, only driven underground. It was decided that it required special people to be employed for the purpose and so the Papal Inquisition first came into existence.

The Dominican order, a preaching order directed against heresy, was chosen for the task. They were known as the 'Hounds of the Lord'. The same period also witnessed the increase of legislation against heresy, and death by burning became the accepted way of dealing with an impenitent heretic.

By the end of the thirteenth century the Papal Inquisition had developed a system of records and officials, and its arm was notoriously long, so that the very mention of the word Inquisition struck terror into every heart. With complete independence, it possessed its own prisons and its activities were clothed in secrecy. The Pope sanctioned the use of torture in 1252. The Inquisitor was to be maintained by the property of the victim – and his property was taken upon arrest. No defence was permitted and the names of accusers were hidden. These were features that would also distinguish the Spanish Inquisition, though that institution developed them to a high pitch of sadistic perfection.

In the middle of the fourteenth century, more than a hundred years before the coming of the Spanish Inquisition, the Kingdom of Castille had been rent apart by a bloody civil war. The substantial Jewish community was made its scapegoats and pogroms had ensued, fanned by zealous Christian preachers. The violence had reached its zenith in 1392 with the murder of hundreds, perhaps thousands of Jews. During this time the Jews had been offered the chance to convert to Christianity. Many had accepted and became known as *conversos*. But the prevalent belief was that they still practised their faith in secret. The *Conversos* provoked suspicion and mistrust, and most believed, 'Jews to be more their neighbours than Christians.' Despite the prejudice around them, many Jews rose to prominence in the royal administration, civic bureaucracy and even the Church. In 1390 the Rabbi of Burgos, who had converted to Catholicism, ended his life as Bishop of Burgos, Papal Legate and tutor to a Prince of the Blood. He was not alone. In some of the major cities, Jews dominated the administration and merchant class. King Ferdinand's treasurer was a *converso*. Three of Isabella's secretaries were *conversos*, as was the official court chronicler.

One of Torquemada's own uncles was a *converso*. They tended to be amongst the best-educated people in Spain, and as they established themselves in business and society, their success and wealth provoked envy and resentment. Their wealth was also to exacerbate the hostility of the Inquisition.

With the advance of the fifteenth century, clerical zealots and political failures began to agitate for the introduction of the Inquisitorial system to cope with the 'problem' of the *conversos*. The first minister to attempt to bring proceedings against them was the unpopular minister Alvaro de Luna. He found himself opposed by two bishops of Jewish extraction but managed to obtain, from Pope Nicholas, a series of Inquisitorial powers to discipline high ecclesiastical figures. But Luna never got the chance to use his powers – he was decapitated in 1453. Then, during the reign of King Henry IV, the agitation assumed a more menacing form. Under the influence of Alonso de Spina, the most learned anti-Semite of the fifteenth century, the Franciscans ordered the introduction of a tribunal to deal with the 'Jewish Problem', which apparently, was growing more serious day by day. But the *conversos* had their supporters and General Fray Alonso de Oropesa mounted the pulpit in their defence. The Franciscans were silenced for the moment, although feelings of bitterness continued. It was the nobility that revived the agitation. In 1464, in the Concordat of Medina del Campo, the king was forced to establish an inquiry into the conduct of the conversos and to punish any that had slipped back into the Jewish faith.

In 1465 Isabella came to the throne amid a blaze of civil war. She was surrounded by ecclesiastics and nobility who were constantly reminding her that steps needed to be taken against the *conversos*, on either political or spiritual grounds. Chief among them was Dominican friar, Tomás de Torquemada. Born at Valladolid in 1420, he was now at the height of his extraordinary powers. He had been the Queen's confessor when she was the Infanta and hated Jews, in spite of, or perhaps because, he was of Jewish extraction. Torquemada's influence over the Queen was enormous and they shared one obsession – to stamp out heresy. As far as Torquemada was concerned the real heretics were not the Jews or Muslims, but the *conversos*, whom he suspected were not true to the Catholic faith.

It was reported that Torquemada had made Isabella take a vow that, should she reach the throne, she would devote herself heart and soul to the extirpation of heresy and the persecution of the Jews. At the time of the oath, it had been unlikely that she would attain the throne, but she had, and Torquemada rose with her.

In 1477 the civil war ended and Isabella went to Seville for a year, where she summoned a national council to discuss Church reforms. The sight of the *conversos*, many of whom were very powerful at court, stimulated Torquemada and Alonso de Hojeda, a vehement anti-Semite, to fresh efforts and condemnations. But Isabella was hesitant, as many of her advisers and courtiers were Jewish. However, on the night of Wednesday 18 March 1478, all this was to change. A young man, in love with a young Jewess, sneaked into her house and surprised a number of *conversos* celebrating Seder. By coincidence it also happened to be Holy Week. A report that the heretics were gathered in order to blaspheme the Christian religion spread across Seville like wildfire. Hojeda and Torquemada hastened to court to tell the Queen of this outrage and she finally decided to take action. A Papal Bull (an edict of the Pope) was demanded from Pope Sixtus IV and eventually issued giving the Spanish sovereigns the right to appoint two Inquisitors to root out heresy in the Kingdom of Castile. The Spanish Inquisition was born and finally, on 7 September 1480, a Seville tribunal was inaugurated. Miguel de Morillo and Juan de San Martin, both Dominicans, were appointed and told to get to work. An alleged conspiracy of Seville's leading *conversos* was soon unearthed and on 6 February 1481, the first *auto-da-fé* (act of the faith) took place. Six men and women were burned alive. A *quemadero*, or place of burning, was constructed just outside the city walls. At the four corners, huge plaster figures of the four major prophets had been erected.

As the news spread of the establishment of the Inquisition many *conversos* fled from Seville into the surrounding countryside. The Inquisition ordered that they be returned and most demands were obeyed, such was the fear engendered by the tribunals. The Marquis of Cadiz returned over 8,000 and the Inquisition's dungeons were soon so full that everyone had to move to the great Castle of Triana, outside the city walls. Despite plague ravaging the city, the *auto-da-fé* continued without interruption. Even the dead were not spared; their bones were exhumed and burnt. By 4 November, 298 people had been burned and 98 condemned to perpetual imprisonment.

Four months later, in February 1482, the Pope authorized the appointment of another seven Dominicans as Inquisitors. One of them, the prior of a monastery in Segovia, was to pass into history as the very embodiment of the Spanish Inquisition at its most terrifying – Tomás de Torquemada. He had previously been content with being the power behind the throne, but his fanatical devotion to his religion made Torquemada the perfect candidate for the position of Inquisitor, and with the support of the Crown, he began to hunt down the *converso* heretics. In the three years following his appointment, tribunals of the Inquisition were established in four other locations and by 1492, tribunals were operating in eight major cities. However, by that point, complaints had begun pouring in from Spanish bishops and, responding to these, the Pope issued a Bull expressing his outrage that so many, 'true and faithful Christians, on the testimony of enemies, rivals, slaves have, without any legitimate proof, been thrust into secular prisons, tortured and condemned...deprived of their goods and property, and handed over to the secular arm to be executed.'

Pointing out that the Inquisition was not solely to deal with the *conversos*, the Pope revoked all the powers of the Inquisition. But the decision to keep or annul Spain's Inquisitors was not the Pope's – and the Bull was seen as a flagrant challenge to the monarchy. Predictably, King Ferdinand and Queen Isabella were outraged.

Confronted by the King's defiance the Pope capitulated completely. On 17 October 1483, a new Bull was issued, which established the *Consejo de la Suprema y General Inquisicion* to function as the Inquisition's ultimate authority. To preside over this council, *La Suprema*, the new office of Inquisitor General was created. Its first incumbent was Torquemada. All the Inquisition tribunals throughout Christian Spain were now under one centralized administration, with Torquemada at its head. Under his direction, the Inquisition rapidly took shape, and extended its activity throughout the country. It was owing to his personal zeal that verdicts of acquittal were infrequent, and over three-quarters of those who perished under the Inquisition in the first 300 years of its existence, did so in the first two decades.

Torquemada became obsessed with the purity of lineage and devised the *Limpreza de Sangre*, or purity of blood document. Anyone with any Jewish blood was prohibited from holding public office or denounced as a heretic. The zenith of Torquemada's activities in Castille was reached when he took proceedings out against a prelate of high character and great learning, who happened to be of Jewish descent. One of the charges brought was that the unfortunate Bishop of Segovia had had the remains of his forebears exhumed, in order to destroy proof that they had been interred with Jewish rites. He was sent to Rome for trial and died a prisoner in the Vatican castle of St Angelo. Torquemada's accusations had been based on nothing but spite.

In the city of Ciudad alone, the Tribunal (in the two years of its existence) burnt fifty-two heretics and condemned 220 fugitives, as well as sentencing 183 people to perform public penance. By 1485 the Tribunal had been transferred to Toledo, where some 750 people took part in the first *auto-da-fé*. Carrying unlit tapers and surrounded by a howling mob, which had flooded in from the surrounding countryside, the accused were compelled to march bareheaded and barefoot through the city to the door of the cathedral. They were fined one-fifth of their property, banned from public office and only allowed to wear the coarsest of clothes. In addition they were also required to go in procession on six successive Fridays, flagellating themselves with hempen cords. At the second *auto-da-fé*, 900 penitents appeared, and there were 750 at the third. Before the end of the year, the total figure had reached 5,000. Large numbers, sometimes fifty a day, were burned, and among the victims were several friars and ecclesiastical dignitaries.

Torquemada produced a handbook of instructions detailing how the secret Jews were to be identified. People were instructed to watch for *conversos* washing their hands before prayer, changing linen on the Sabbath and shopping in Jewish stores. Wholesale denunciations were encouraged by a promise of a free pardon in return for full confession, which placed thousands in the power of the dreaded Tribunal. Inquisitors had two manuals at their disposal on how to deal with heretics. The first, *The Practice of the Office of the Inquisition of Heretical Depravity*, was composed in 1324. The second was the *Inquisitors Directory* by Nicholas Eymerich. Both identified Jews as particularly dangerous for Christian society and *conversos* as the most dangerous of all.

When Torqemada's train of death appeared, city gates were flung open, the resources of the city were placed at his disposal and magistrates swore him their devotion. The Inquisition would descend on a town or village at regular intervals and Inquisitors present themselves to the local church and civic authorities. A day would be proclaimed and everyone would be compelled to attend a special Mass to hear the Inquisition's 'Edict' read in public. On the appointed day, at the end of the sermon, the Inquisitor would raise a crucifix. Those in attendance would be required to raise their right hands, cross themselves and repeat an oath to support the Inquisition and its servants.

The edict listed various heresies, as well as support of Islam and Judaism, and called forward all those who might be guilty of infraction. If they confessed themselves within a stipulated period of grace – generally thirty to forty days, although being at the Inquisitor's discretion, it was often less – they might be accepted back into the Church and allowed to get away with doing penance. They would be required to renounce any guilty parties who had not come forward. Indeed, this was a crucial pre-requisite for being allowed to escape with nothing more severe than a penance. For the Inquisition, 'a convert who would betray his friends was more useful than a roasted corpse.'

In Spain, as elsewhere, people would avail themselves of the Inquisition to settle old scores, to exact personal vengeance on neighbours and relatives, and to eliminate business rivals. Anyone could denounce anyone else, and the burden of vindication would lie with the accused. Increasingly, people began to fear their neighbours, their business associates, in fact anyone whom they may have antagonized. They would also often bear false witness against themselves, sometimes confessing en masse, submitting themselves to the paranoia and dread that the Inquisition provoked.

Petty denunciations were the rule rather than the exception. In Castille during the 1480s, over 1,500 people were burnt at the stake as a result of false testimony, often unable even to determine whom their accusers were. Witnesses in investigations were kept anonymous, and their testimonies edited for any items that might betray their identities.

The Inquisition derived its energy and impetus from the very population it persecuted, its power stemming from a blatant exploitation of the weakest and most venal aspects of human nature. In theory, each case was to be examined by a conclave of theologians – the visiting Inquisitor and at least one local – but in practice many people were arrested before their cases were assessed. The Inquisition's prisons were crammed with people waiting to hear the charges against them, and they could be kept for years without knowing why. In the meantime, they and their families would have been stripped of all their property, for an arrest was always accompanied by the immediate confiscation of all the accused's belongings – everything from the house down to pots and pans. While in prison, the accused's property could be sold off to pay for his maintenance in captivity. When eventually released, he could find himself bankrupt or destitute. Children of prisoners are recorded as having died from starvation.

Even the most lenient of punishments, the penance, could be severe. The lightest penalty was 'discipline'. The self-confessed heretic would be obliged each Sunday to strip and appear in church carrying a rod. At a certain time in the Mass, the priest would energetically whip the victim before the entire congregation – a fitting interlude in the divine service. Punishment did not end there. On the first Sunday of every month, the penitent would be compelled to visit every house in which he had met with other heretics, and in each, would be whipped again. On feast days, he would be required to follow the procession and then be whipped again. These ordeals were inflicted for the rest of his life, unless released from the penance by the Inquisitor on a return visit.

Another form of penance was the pilgrimage. Taken on foot these could often take several years, during which time a man's family might well starve. Pilgrimages could be to holy shrines or as far afield as Jerusalem. Confessed heretics might also be compelled to wear, for the rest of their lives, a large saffron cross sewn on the breast and back of all their garments. The penitent was then exposed to constant social humiliation, ridicule and violence.

Penance could also take the form of a fine. Such fines quickly became a source of scandal since Inquisitors often extorted large sums of money for themselves. The Inquisition was financed by money and goods obtained from their victims, and bribery and corruption were rife. In 1499, the Inquisitor of Cordoba was convicted of fraud and extortion. His successor blithely followed in his footsteps. Torquemada himself, despite his vow of poverty, accumulated vast wealth.

Death afforded no release. If the penitent was not judged to have sufficiently atoned, then his bones were dug up and burnt, and his family could become liable for his penances and his debts. If the accused chose to run, his body was burnt in effigy, but if the person accused of heresy did not flee, and the charges were deemed sufficient, they were arrested and put into the hands of the Inquisitors. Since no Inquisitor cared to be wrong, every possible subterfuge was used to extract or extort a confession. One Inquisitor remarked that 'there is no need for haste, for the pains and privation of imprisonment often bring about a change of mind.' Inquisitors were licensed by the Pope to carry out torture, preferably without shedding blood, and new methods of torture were invented to aid this hypocrisy. The rack, thumbscrews and other devices that caused blood to flow only 'incidentally' were favoured. Pincers and other such toys had to be white hot so that the heated metal would cauterize the wound, as the flesh was being torn open.

There was *toca*, or water torture, when water was forced down a victim's throat. There was *potro*, when the person was bound to a rack by tight cords that could be tightened further and further. Then there was *garrucha*, in which the heretic would be hung by the wrists from a pulley in the ceiling with weights fastened to his or her feet. Raising the pulley slowly, to maximize the pain, they would then be dropped a few feet abruptly, dislocating the limbs. It was certainly not unusual for a death to occur, but this was always deemed to have been accidental and not as a result of the torture.

The Inquisition realized that confessions under torture did not carry a great deal of weight – under severe pain people will say anything. The victims were therefore made to confirm the statement a couple of days later, so that the confession could be labelled 'not under duress'. Technically the Inquisition was only meant to torture once, but this was circumvented by describing the end of each session as a 'suspension'.

In administering the death sentence, clerical hypocrisy displayed itself again. Inquisitors could not themselves perform executions, which might have made them appear un-Christian. Instead they were obliged to enact the ritual whereby they handed the heretic over to the secular authorities so they could do the deed for them. To ensure the maximum number of spectators, executions were performed on public holidays. The condemned would be tied to a pyre of dry wood, located well above the crowd to ensure a good view. When they were dead, the body was separated into pieces, the bones were broken and everything was thrown onto a fresh fire.

Before the marriage of Ferdinand and Isabella, Spain had been a divided country. Under their joint rule the two kingdoms of Aragon and Castille were united. Now King Ferdinand wanted to establish an Inquisition in Aragon, but he had to petition the Pope to get rid of the existing tribunals, which had been set up in the thirteenth century. Having never been keen on issuing the original Bull to Isabella for Castille in 1478, the Pope initially objected to authorizing the entry of the Inquisition to Aragon. Finally, however, after a great deal of double-dealing, Torquemada, the Castillian Inquisitor General, was granted the right to appoint Inquisitors in Aragon, Catalonia and Valencia. Torquemada's appointment, overriding the complete legal and constitutional separation between Castille and Aragon, created a storm, which engulfed hundreds of people, in addition to the *conversos*.

Violent opposition broke out against Ferdinand's Inquisition as the *conversos* fought to be recognized as sincere Christians. *Autos-da-fé* had already taken place in Castille and Andalusia, and stories abounded of the arbitrary cruelty committed by the Inquisitors. The Aragonese and Catalonian *conversos* had little doubt concerning the fate that awaited them once Torquemada's Inquisitors arrived, which they did on 14 April 1484. However, the *conversos* of Aragon were well organized, rich and powerful, and determined not to give way without resistance. It was in Saragossa, the capital of Aragon, that they struck back hardest.

The Inquisitor of Saragossa was Pedro Arbues. Aware that his life was in danger, he had taken to wearing full chain mail beneath his vestments, but four prominent *conversos*, including the Master of the Royal Household and High Treasurer of the Kingdom, hired assassins, and on the night of 15 September 1485, Arbues was stabbed to death while kneeling in prayer at the cathedral's altar. When the identity of the assassins was discovered, the whole mood of Saragossa changed, and with it that of Aragon.

Arbues was declared a saint, miracles were worked with his blood, and mobs roamed the streets in search of *conversos*. One of the plotters had his hands cut off and nailed to the door of the court house, after which he was dragged to the market-place, beheaded and quartered, and the pieces of his body suspended in the streets of the city. Another committed suicide in his cell by swallowing a broken glass lamp; his dead body treated in the same manner as that of his fellow plotter.

Hundreds of people were arrested and thrown into the dungeons of the Aljaferia, the old Moorish fortress – as many as forty to a single cell, devoid of the most basic amenities. Over 200 were burnt and a large number of Aragon's *conversos* fell into in the hands of the Inquisition. One retaliatory murder had turned out to provoke an act of mass suicide that annihilated all opposition to the Inquisition for the next one hundred years.

In 1488 the Inquisition spread to Barcelona, and the following year the island of Majorca came under the lash. Flight to foreign countries, especially the south of France, began to assume panic proportions. But for many there was to be no escape and Pope Innocent VIII ordered them to be handed back. Hundreds were returned, back into the waiting arms of Torquemada.

From the moment of its creation, the Spanish Inquisition had cast covetous eyes on Judaic wealth, but initially they could not seize it. The Inquisition was charged to deal with heretics i.e. Christians who had deviated from the orthodox ideals of the faith; it had no powers over different religions. So a large percentage of the population remained outside its control, but it was a situation that was not to last long.

By the end of the 1480s Torquemada had realized that the greatest threat to the purity of the Catholic Church came from practising Jews, and so the Inquisition now embarked on an anti-Semitic propaganda campaign. Extraordinary accusations would be made and repeated time after time, until they would eventually come to be accepted as valid. Managing to provoke the population, the Inquisition now petitioned the Crown to adopt the necessary measures. Initially, however, Ferdinand and Isabella demurred. They needed Jewish money to fight to regain the city of Granada, the last stronghold of the Moors and Islam. Until the whole of Spain was reconciled to Catholicism, the expulsion of the Jews would have to wait. However, with the recapture of Granada from the Moors in 1492, the religious zeal of the Spanish Inquisition was given free reign. In the flush of victory, there seemed to be no reason why practising Jews should be tolerated. The Inquisition had not been able to get its hands on them before – they were not heretics within the

Church but infidels outside it, over whom no clerical tribunal had jurisdiction. It was a somewhat ridiculous situation. A *converso*, forced into baptism with a dagger at his throat, would be burned alive for following the Jewish faith in secret, while the unconverted Jew could practice with impunity. In addition, the Inquisition reasoned, the *conversos* were corrupted by the presence of practising Jews. All Torquemada had to do was find an excuse to get rid of them.

On 14 November 1491, two weeks before the fall of Granada, five Jews and six *conversos* were sent to the stake in Avila. Accused of crucifying a Christian child and ripping its heart out, they had supposedly been performing a magical rite designed to disable the Inquisition and send all Christians, 'raving mad to their deaths'. The Inquisition made sure that every city in Spain came to hear of it, and anti-Semitic fury rose to a peak. Torquemada took the story before Ferdinand and Isabella as proof of the complicity between Jews and *conversos*.

Under appeal from Abraham Signor, a Jewish courtier who had helped arrange their marriage, Ferdinand and Isabella wavered about expelling the Jews. Signor offered them a tremendous amount of gold in exchange for the Jews being able to stay. When he heard this, Torquemada burst into the royal chambers and threw thirty pieces of silver at the King and Queen, reminding them that Judas had sold Christ for the same amount and that they were selling him out again.

On 30 March 1492, Ferdinand and Isabella, in their council chamber at the captured Alhambra in Granada, signed the decree which drove into exile 200,000 loyal Jewish Spaniards, whose ancestors had lived in the country since time immemorial. Four months later, the last Jews had departed, and the great dream of Torquemada's life had been realized. The *conversos* were now completely alone. The task of the Inquisition was simplified – there was now a clean-cut division between the unconverted Jew and the converted. The former had gone into exile; the relatively simple task remained of forcing the latter into conformity.

Six years later, Tomás de Torquemada died peacefully in his monastery in Avila in the odour of sanctity. He had been responsible for thousands of deaths and the eradication of Judaism in Spain – just as Hitler was to do throughout Europe, almost 450 years later. He was succeeded as Grand Inquisitor by the scholarly Diego Diez. With Isabella's death in 1504, the Inquisition lost its state support, but would remain in existence for another 300 years. Its last victim, a schoolteacher from Rusafa, was burnt alive in 1824. The Inquisition still exists today under the name 'The Congregation for the Doctrine of Faith'. It still has the power to silence and excommunicate dissident Catholics.

PRINCE VLAD DRACULA

'THE IMPALER'

The character [of Dracula] originates from a fifteenth-century prince of Wallachia in Romania, Vlad V, whose nickname was 'the Impaler' owing to his beastly little habit of slowly impaling the Turkish invaders of his country and drinking their blood with his dinner. The name 'Dracula' derives from his father, who was known as Vlad Dracul (he Devil), and Castle Dracula in the Carpathian Mountains, north of Bucharest.

PETER CUSHING, INTRODUCTION TO
VAMPIRE STORIES (1992)

From the ancient Kingdom of Wallachia, in what is now modern Romania, a man emerged who would become renowned for devising innovative methods of torture and execution. Vlad Tepes Dracula, Prince of Wallachia, conquered and lost the throne of Wallachia three times in his life. Over his bloody, seven-year reign, he brought terror to citizens and foreigners alike. He was a ruler whose obsession with loyalty would lead to a murderous paranoia and the death of more than 100,000 people. If Dracula ever walked the earth as a creature of flesh and blood rather than as a figure of fiction, then the person who deserved the title was Vlad Tepes. But the legend of Count Dracula is a fairy tale compared with the catalogue of terror, torture and sheer blood lust that marked the violent life of the Wallachian Prince – otherwise known as Vlad the Impaler.

A Transylvanian called Radu Negru, or Rudolph the Black, had founded Wallachia in 1290. Hungary dominated Wallachia until 1330, when it became independent. The first ruler of the country was Prince Basarab the Great (1310-52), an ancestor of Vlad the Impaler. Vlad's grandfather, Prince Mircea the Old, reigned from 1386-1418, and it was during his reign that

Wallachia was forced to pay tribute to the Turkish Ottoman Empire. The family continued to rule Wallachia, but as vassals of the Turks.

Wallachia was wracked by unrest and instability; it was threatened from the outside by the Turkish Ottoman Empire and from within by a corrupt boyar (a member of the old Russian aristocracy).

Vlad's father, Dracul, was educated in Hungary and Germany, and served as a page of King Sigismund of Hungary, who became the Holy Roman Emperor in 1410. Sigismund founded a secret order of knights called the Order of the Dragon, and Dracul was invited to join the brotherhood. This was a secret military and religious confraternity, to protect the Christian Church against heretics and organize crusades against the Turks, who had overrun most of the Balkan Peninsula. Eventually, Sigismund appointed Dracul as military governor of Transylvania, a post he held for four years until 1435. Vlad was born in the military fortress of Sighisoara in 1431. He was the second son of Vlad Dracul and Princess Cneajna of Moldavia. He had an older brother, Mircea, and a younger brother, Radu the Handsome.

From an early age, the young Vlad developed a taste for death. Much of his spare time was spent watching criminals being led to their execution at his father's court in the royal capital of Tirgoviste, and by the age of five, Vlad was being prepared for war. He galloped bareback, was a good shot with his bow and arrow, and was initiated into the Order of the Dragon, and given the name Dracula, meaning son of Dracul.

But Vlad's father, having served as military governor for some time, decided he was not content to remain one forever. During his years in Transylvania, he gathered supporters to help him seize the Wallachian throne from Alexandru I. In 1437 Vlad Dracul killed Alexandru and became Prince Vlad II.

Dracul, a wily politician, sensed that the balance of power was shifting in favour of the ambitious new Sultan Mehmed II – the Turks had recently destroyed both the Serbs and Bulgars and were contemplating a final blow against the Greeks. Dracul signed an alliance with the Sultan.

Despite his treachery, the Wallachians were happier to be ruled by one of their own kind than the Turks. Dracul tried to prevent some of the Turks' worst excesses, in particular their fondness for carrying off slaves, and this made the Sultan suspicious, so he tricked Dracul into a personal confrontation and, impervious to the snare, Dracul crossed the Danube with Vlad and his youngest son, Radu. Dracul was captured and bound in iron chains, and brought before the Sultan. In order to save himself and regain his throne, Dracul swore fidelity to Mehmed II and left both Vlad and Radu as hostages.

Vlad remained a Turkish captive until 1448; Radu stayed on and became the ally of Mehmed II and, because of his weaker nature, submitted more easily to the refined indoctrination technique of his jailers.

Vlad's reaction to these dangerous years was quite the reverse. From the moment of his imprisonment in Turkey, Vlad held human nature in low esteem. Life was cheap – after all his own life was in danger, should his father prove disloyal to the Sultan – and morality was not essential in matters of state. The Turks taught Vlad their language as well as acquainting him with the pleasures of the harem – the terms of confinement were not too strict. He also developed a reputation for trickery, cunning, insubordination and brutality, and inspired terror in his own guards. He became fascinated by impalement and its use as a deterrent in psychological warfare. He was also introduced to gunpowder and its use in cannons for warfare, and would become one of the first leaders to use gunpowder in combat.

He developed two other personality traits: he was suspicious – never again would he allow himself to trust the Turks or any man – and he discovered a taste for revenge. Vlad would not forgive, or forget, those who crossed him.

In December 1447, Dracul died, a victim of his own plotting. His murder was organized by John Hunyadi, the leader of the Hungarians, who had become angered by Dracul's alliance with the Turks. Dracul's eldest son, Mircea, was blinded with red-hot iron stakes and buried alive by his political enemies in Tirgoviste. Dracul's assassination took place in the marshes of Balteni, near an ancient monastery.

These killings, not suprisingly, had a profound effect on Vlad, and he swore he would get his revenge.

Since Dracul and Mircea were dead, and Vlad and Radu were in Turkey, Hunyadi was able to put a member of the Danesti clan, Vladislav II, on the Wallachian throne. But the Turks were opposed to having a Hungarian puppet in charge of Wallachia, so in 1448 they freed Vlad, whom they believed had finally been subdued. Supported by a force of Turkish cavalry and a contingent of troops lent to him by Pasha Mustafa Hassan, Vlad made his first move towards seizing the Wallachian throne. He was seventeen years of age.

The bold coup succeeded for nearly two months, until Hunyadi forced Vlad once more into exile, and reinstated Vladislav II. Vlad, fearful of his father's assassins and equally reluctant to return to his Turkish captors, fled to Moldavia, the northernmost Romanian principality, where his cousin and friend, Prince Stephen, was heir to the throne.

Vlad stayed in Moldavia until October 1451, then reappeared in Transylvania and threw himself on Hunyadi's mercy. Though he was taking a chance, his timing was perfect. Vladislav II had recently changed sides and declared his allegiance to the Turks, and Hunyadi had begun to regret having restored him to the throne and was now seeking a replacement. Vlad became the official claimant to the Wallachian throne and Hunyadi introduced his protégé to the court of the Hapsburg King in Hungary. Vlad took part in many of Hunyadi's campaigns against the Turks, and he could have had no finer instruction in anti-Turkish strategy.

In 1456 Halley's Comet appeared in the sky – 'as long as half the sky with two tails, one pointing west, the other east, coloured gold and looking like an undulated flame'. In the fifteenth century, superstitious people looked upon the comet as a warning of natural catastrophes, plagues or threat of invasion. They were right. In the same year Vlad killed Vladislav II and regained the throne. Now Prince Vlad II Dracula began his infamous and bloody reign.

At twenty-five years old, he was the very picture of a prince, dressed in a rich sable coat with gold brocade, topped off with a flamboyant red silk hat laced with pearls. His face was sallow, with large, green, penetrating eyes, surrounded by deep, dark shadows – his bushy black eyebrows making his eyes appear even more threatening. Vlad boasted a fashionable moustache, which he meticulously twisted at the ends. He was not tall, but very stocky and strong. His nostrils were flared and he had a strong, aquiline nose. His appearance was cold, distant and unmistakably powerful.

Vlad's immediate priority was to consolidate his position in Wallachia. He was determined to defend his country against foreign invasion, in addition to which he wanted to break the political power of the boyars. Vlad was also faced with the continuous threat from rival claimants to the throne and so, once in power, he rebuilt his fortresses' defences by constructing thick battlements, watchtowers and underground tunnels. He then turned to ensuring the loyalty of his subjects. Vlad began by employing a technique the Turks had taught him as a young man – impalement. In his hands, impalement became an art-form, the special knowledge and particular skill it took to carry out a successful impalement appealing to Vlad's meticulous nature. Vlad usually had a horse attached to each of the victim's legs, and a sharpened stake of between six and eight feet in height and about six inches wide was gradually forced up vertically through the body. The end of the stake was usually oiled, and care was taken that the stake was not too sharp, or else the victim might die too rapidly from shock. The stake normally started at the buttocks and was worked out through the mouth, but sometimes it was just stabbed through the victim's chest or stomach. Sometimes people were hung upside down, and babies were impaled on the stakes that killed their mothers. The stake was then turned upright and planted in the ground – the longer the stake, the more important the victim. One nobleman, who wrinkled his nose as he dined with Vlad in a courtyard of cadavers, was given an extra long stake to put him above the stench of those impaled around him. The stakes were also often elaborately carved and painted, and Vlad displayed the impaled bodies on the outskirts of the city as a warning to foreigners to stay away. As it would sometimes take days for the victims to die, the pungent smell of death was always in the air.

Vlad also enjoyed experimenting with other forms of torture. He had a large pot made with boards fastened over it – people's heads were put through the holes and trapped there. Then he had the pot filled with water and a large fire made underneath. He relished the screams of agony as his victims were boiled alive.

In the year 1460, on the morning of St Bartholomew's Day, Vlad came through a forest to the village of Amlas, where the residents were suspected of supporting a rival. He had all the Wallachians, of both sexes, tracked down and cut to ribbons with swords, sabres and knives – it is rumoured that over 30,000 lost their lives. The chaplain and influential people of the village were taken back to his capital and impaled. He then burnt the town out of existence.

Vlad was also determined to break the economic hold that the Saxon merchants of southern Transylvania had on trade in the country. Not only were these merchants ignoring custom duty, they were also supporting rival claimants to the throne and so, when local merchants in Brasov refused to pay Vlad's taxes, in spite of repeated warnings, Vlad led an assault on the town. He burnt an entire suburb and impaled numerous captives on Timpa Hill. Brasov has the distinction of having witnessed on its surrounding hills more stakes bearing Vlad's victims rotting in the sun, or chewed and mangled by Carpathian vultures, than any other place in the principality. The scene has been immortalized on a particularly gruesome woodcut printed in Nuremberg around 1499. It depicts Vlad eating a meal, while impaled victims are dying around him. As he dines, his henchmen are hacking off limbs of other victims right next to his table. Similar woodcuts appeared throughout Europe; in fact, some of the earliest secular texts to roll off the recently invented printing press, were about Vlad the Impaler's activities. Most are tales of horror with some sort of moral for the reader. Though distortion is unquestionable, their amazing accuracy of historical, geographical and topographical detail has led scholars to accept many of them as accurate.

Tirgoviste, Wallachia's capital, was not just a seat of power, but also the nation's centre of social and cultural life. The royal palace was ostentatious and surrounded by the Byzantine-style houses of the boyars, where the upper class attempted to ape the etiquette of the imperial court of Constantinople. Suspicion reigned in the capital; anarchy was rampant, political assassination was frequent, and the rapid succession of princes was the rule rather than the exception. Having perfected his preferred instrument of torture, Vlad's first major act of revenge was now aimed at the nobles of Tirgoviste, whom he held responsible for the deaths of his father and brother, Mircea.

In the spring of 1457, he invited the rich landowners and their families, along with the five bishops, the abbots of the more important foreign and native monasteries, and the archbishop, to an Easter banquet at the palace. As Vlad surveyed the wily, dishonest expressions of the boyars, he asked them how many reigns they had lived through – even the young men admitted to having been through at least seven. The princely title and all that it implied had evidently been taken lightly. Vlad began shouting furiously, blaming the instability of the Wallachian throne on their disloyalty and plotting. Then, his eyes flashing in a way that would become characteristic, the order was given. Within minutes, his faithful attendants had surrounded the hall. Some 500 boyars, their wives and attendants were immediately impaled in the vicinity of the palace and left exposed until the birds devoured their corpses. The lesson was not lost on the remaining boyars – Vlad was demanding their total submission or exile to their estates. Woe to him who chose to disobey.

Prince Vlad also seized his victims' property and passed it out to his supporters. He was creating a new nobility, loyal only to him.

He now became increasingly concerned that all his subjects should work and contribute to the common welfare. He noticed that the vagrants, beggars and cripples had become extremely numerous. He issued an invitation to all the poor and sick in Wallachia to come to Tirgoviste for a great feast, claiming that no one should go hungry in his land. As the poor and crippled arrived, they were ushered into a great hall where a fabulous feast was prepared for them.

The prince's guests ate and drank late into the night, when Vlad himself made an appearance. 'What else do you desire? Do you want to be without cares, lacking nothing in this world?' asked the Prince. When they responded positively, Vlad ordered that the hall be boarded up and set on fire. None escaped the flames. Vlad justified his actions by claiming that it was necessary so that 'they represented no further burden to others.'

Vlad now instigated a strict moral code. Thieves, liars, adulterers and even children were impaled. He killed merchants who cheated their customers, and women who had affairs. A visiting merchant once left his money outside all night, thinking that it would be safe because of Vlad's draconian policies. To his surprise, some of the coins were stolen. He complained to Vlad, who promptly issued a proclamation that the money must be returned or the city would be destroyed. That night, Vlad secretly had the missing money, plus one extra coin, returned to the merchant. The next morning the merchant found the money and counted it. He told Vlad the money had been returned, and mentioned the extra coin. Vlad replied that the thief had been caught and would be impaled, adding that if the merchant hadn't mentioned the extra coin, he would have been impaled too.

Fear of Vlad's wrath ensured that crime was kept to a minimum and, as a sign of his absolute power, he had a gold cup placed in a public square. Anyone was allowed to drink from it, but no one was allowed to move it. The cup remained in the square throughout his reign.

Vlad also liked to make the punishment fit the crime. When Turkish emissaries from the Sultan refused to remove their turbans in his presence, Vlad saw this as an act of rudeness and ordered his guards to seize them, then returned the insult by nailing their hats to their heads.

Just as Vlad reacted violently to insult, he responded very well to flattery. On one occasion a messenger was sent to Vlad from King Matthias of Hungary. It is unknown what news the messenger brought, but it angered Vlad intensely. Vlad invited the messenger to eat dinner with him personally. Before the meal, he asked him if he knew why he had invited him to dinner. The messenger, seeing two soldiers standing behind the Prince, and knowing Vlad's reputation, presumed it meant his imminent death. Thinking quickly, he replied, 'I do not know, but I know you are a wise and great ruler, and no matter what you command, even if you were to command my death, it should be done.' Vlad motioned the soldiers away and told the messenger that his answer had saved his life.

But there were two sides to Vlad's personality. One was the torturer and inquisitor, who used terror deliberately as an instrument of policy; the other was a deeply religious man who had turned to piety to ease his conscience. He took the precaution of surrounding himself with priests, abbots, bishops and confessors, whether Roman Catholic or Orthodox. He meditated within the saintly confines of monasteries, such as Tismana. He was intent on belonging to a church, receiving the sacraments, being buried as a Christian, and being identified with a religion.

Vlad felt that good works, particularly the erection of monasteries, along with rich endowments and an appropriate ritual at the moment of death, would contribute to the eradication of sin. He was most concerned with the survival of the soul in the afterlife. He had particular qualms concerning those victims for whose death he was personally responsible and gave them Christian burials. His family had been responsible for building over forty monasteries, and Vlad built five more.

Of Vlad's romantic life virtually nothing is known. His first wife or mistress was a Transylvanian commoner, with whom he had fallen in love in 1448. The marriage was apparently unhappy. Loving Vlad could be a dangerous thing. When a mistress was caught being unfaithful, she was impaled and had her sexual organs cut out. His last wife threw herself from the battlements of Poenari Castle to avoid being captured by the Turks.

*

The Balkan states were torn apart by dissent – the absence of unity helped the Turkish cause and had contributed to the fall of Constantinople in 1453, three years before Vlad's second accession to the Wallachian throne.

Following the fall of Constantinople, Pope Pius II in 1458 asked Christians to take up the cross and fight the Turks. Vlad was the only one who responded immediately to the Papal plea and his courageous action was rewarded favourably – his cruel tactics may have revolted people, but they praised his willingness to fight for Christianity.

Vlad had only paid his tribute to the Turks for the first three years of his reign. He then further violated his obligation, and failed to appear before the Sultan. The Turks responded by asking for a child tribute – 500 young boys to be handed over for their armies. Turkish recruiting officers had occasionally swept down into Wallachia to obtain good, young men. Vlad resisted such incursions with a force of arms, and any Turk who was caught would be impaled.

Such violations of territory by both sides only further embittered Turkish-Wallachian relations. Raiding, pillaging and looting were endemic from Giurgiu to the Black Sea, and the Sultan had succeeded in securing control of various fortresses and townships on the Romanian side of the Danube. To further complicate matters, Radu the Handsome, Vlad's brother, who had faithfully resided at Constantinople since 1447, was encouraged by the Turks to consider himself as a candidate to the Wallachian throne.

Sultan Mehmed II asked Vlad to meet with his representative, Isaac Pasha, but remembering how his father had been tricked, Vlad refused to go; he was also aware that, if he left the country, his enemies would seize power in his absence. There was no basis for negotiations, and so the Turks laid a plan to ambush Vlad. Knowing that he would never come to Constantinople, their orders were to capture him dead or alive. But Vlad out-foxed his opponents. He captured the Turkish envoy, and tricked the Turks into opening the gates of the city of Giurgiu and, once inside, set the city on fire. Vlad then launched a series of hostilities without actually declaring war. He kept notes on the numbers of deaths. 'I have killed men and women, old and young, who lived at Oblucitza and Novoselo. We killed 23,884 Turks and Bulgars without counting those whom we burned in homes or whose heads were not cut by our soldiers. I have broken peace with the Sultan.'

The campaign ended on the shores of the Black Sea, within sight of the powerful Turkish invasion force that had crossed the Bosporus, on giant barges, for a full-scale invasion of Wallachia. With his flank unprotected, Vlad was compelled to abandon the offensive.

Meanwhile, throughout central and western Europe, church bells tolled from Genoa to Paris in gratitude for Vlad's endowing the crusade with a new lease of life, and taking over the leadership of the great Hunyadi. His bold offensive had given new hopes of liberation to the enslaved people of Bulgaria, Serbia and Greece. At Constantinople, there was an atmosphere of consternation, gloom and fear as some of the Turkish leaders, fearing the Impaler, contemplated flight to Asia Minor.

Mehmed decided to launch an invasion during the spring of 1462 – Vlad had given him no alternative. To defy the Sultan by avoiding an assassination plot was one thing, but to instil hopes of freedom amongst his Christian subjects was quite another. Mehmed was determined to reduce Wallachia to a Turkish province, and amassed the largest Turkish force since the invasion of Constantinople.

Vlad only had 30,900 men and so abandoned his position on the Danube and began his withdrawal northward. The idea was to draw the enemy force deep into his own territory. According to Romanian tradition, the forest and the mountains were brothers of the people that had ensured the survival of Wallachia through the ages.

As the Wallachian troops gave up their native soil, Vlad used scorched-earth tactics, creating a vast desert in the path of the invading army. His men set fire to the cities, reducing them to ghost towns, and depopulated the entire area. Boyars, peasants and townspeople all accompanied the retreating armies, unless they could find refuge in the mountains, where

47

the wealthy sought safety. Vlad ordered the crops to be burnt, poisoned the wells, and destroyed the cattle and all other domestic animals that could not be herded away into the mountains. He ordered huge pits to be dug and covered them with timber and leaves to trap Turkish men, horses and camels. He even ordered the construction of small dams to divert the waters of small rivers to create marshes, thus impeding the progress of the Turkish cannons by miring them down.

In this parched plain, the lips of the fighters for Islam dried up. They used their shields to roast meat. The summer of 1462 was one of the hottest on record. But Vlad knew that to be really effective he would have to kill the Sultan, and so he started to plan.

One evening, Mehmed had retired after a heavy meal, when suddenly came the hooting of an owl, Vlad's signal to attack. Initially, the Turkish army was terrified, but they rallied and surrounded the Sultan's tent. Vlad killed several thousand Turks, wounded countless more, created havoc, chaos and terror, but he lost several hundred of his bravest warriors, and the attack failed. Sultan Mehmed II survived, and the road to Tirgoviste lay open.

When the Turks finally entered the city, they found it denuded, with no cattle, men, food or drink. The gates had been left open and the city was enveloped by a thick blanket of smoke. Mehmed decided to continue his hunt for the elusive Impaler.

Just a few miles to the north, the Sultan caught sight of an even more desolate spectacle: in a narrow gorge, one mile long, he found a forest of impaled cadavers, perhaps 20,000 in all. The Sultan caught sight of the mangled, rotting remains of men, women and children – the flesh being eaten by birds that nestled in the skulls and rib cages. Mehmed found corpses of Turkish warriors caught during the previous winter, and on a higher pike were the bodies of the two assassins who had tried to ensnare Vlad before the war had begun.

Mehmed gave orders for the retreat and started eastward where the fleet was anchored, but, before leaving, he formally appointed Radu as commander-in-chief, and entrusted him with the mission of destroying Vlad and becoming King. A Turkish contingent would remain to support Radu, but the new commander was to rely principally on native support. The boyars, realizing that the Turks were stronger, now abandoned Vlad. Radu pursued his brother all the way to his fortress in Poenari.

When the Turks eventually seized the castle, Vlad was forced to escape through a secret tunnel. Now, another tragedy befell him. The servant carrying Vlad's infant son dropped him. The pursuing Turks were too close to risk turning back to look for the child, so they were forced to leave him behind. In one day, Vlad had lost both his home and his family. Vlad and his servants escaped through the forest on horseback.

Seeking help near Brasov, Vlad now went to King Matthias of Hungary, but his evil deeds had finally caught up with him. Brasov contained a large number of the German merchants that Vlad had been terrorizing for the past few years. They had got to the Hungarian court first, and told Matthias that Vlad was an ally of the Turks and that he was coming to the King as a spy. When Vlad arrived, he was immediately thrown into prison.

However, Matthias was in a difficult situation. Vlad's standing in much of Europe was very high at the time and Matthias had to produce a convincing reason for capturing Vlad. A series of letters were forged, which claimed that Vlad had subjugated himself entirely to the Sultan's wishes.

Matthias now had a valid pretext for giving up the campaign and breaking his alliance with Vlad, enabling him to keep the Papal subsidies for his own political ambitions. Matthias signed a secret agreement with Sultan Mehmed and recognized Radu as Prince of Wallachia. Without the formality of a trial, Vlad now had to undergo a lengthy period of imprisonment, but luck was on his side in the shape of Iona, King Matthias's sister, whose eye Vlad had caught, who used her influence with her brother to have Vlad freed. Subsequently, Iona and Vlad were married and, after four years, Vlad was partially pardoned, although he was required to stay within the city. With no subjects to torture, he impaled rats and birds for fun.

Vlad spent the next twelve years plotting his return to the throne, and gaining the trust of his jailer, King Matthias. Vlad's marriage into the King's family re-established the status quo. Vlad was given the title of Captain, and the king prepared him for a crusade against the Turks.

The Turks had not stayed long in Wallachia. The impaled heads of several of their spies had greeted them, and Vlad had burned the city of Tirgoviste. After only a few days, the Black Plague broke out among the Turkish soldiers, and they were forced to retreat, leaving Radu behind. Vlad watched and waited, while Radu ruled Wallachia as a puppet of the Turks. Finally, in 1473, Radu was defeated – his successor was Basarab III, who was deemed totally unsuitable by the Hungarians.

In 1475, a formal treaty was signed between Hungaria, Moldavia and Vlad, and Vlad seized the throne for the third and final time. But he had many enemies, and when his allies left Wallachia, he was extremely vulnerable. His failure to bring his wife and sons with him to Wallachia suggests that he was well aware of the danger. Now the only people he could trust was a small band of 200 soldiers.

In late December 1476, near the monastery of Snagov in the Vlasia forest near Bucharest, Vlad and his force were out killing the Turks. Out of sheer joy, Vlad ascended a hill in order to see his men massacring the Sultan's troops. Detached from his army, Vlad was struck by a lance. He defended himself formidably, killing five of his assassins, but to no avail. Finally, he was killed and his severed head was sent to Constantinople, where it was impaled on a high stake for the population to witness that the great Impaler had himself been impaled.

After Vlad's death, his wife was left with his three sons. His eldest, Mihnea, from Vlad's union with a Transylvanian noblewoman, finally succeeded to the Wallachian throne. During his brief one-year rule in 1508, he showed signs that he could be as atrocious as his infamous father. Nicknamed Mihnea the Bad, he is reputed to have cut off the noses and lips of his political enemies. He was assassinated in 1510, on the steps of a church in Sibiu.

FRANCISCO PIZARRO

'CONQUEROR OF THE INCAS'

> He [Atahualpa] one day told Pizarro that, if he would set him
> free, he would cover the floor of the apartment in which they
> stood with gold. Those present listened with an incredulous
> smile; and, as the Inca received no answer, he said with some
> emphasis that 'he would not merely cover the floor, but would
> fill the room with gold as high as he could reach'.
>
> WILLIAM H. PRESCOTT, HISTORY OF THE CONQUEST OF
> PERU, WITH A PRELIMINARY VIEW OF THE
> CIVILIZATION OF THE INCAS (1847)

Francisco Pizarro, a peasant from Spain, was one of the least
well-equipped conquerors in history. In the name of Christ,
he destroyed the powerful Empire of the Incas and bestowed
on Spain the richest of possessions. Pizarro also established the
city of Lima in Peru, thus opening the way for Spanish culture
to dominate South America.

In 1493, in order to prevent a war between Spain and
Portugal over discoveries in the New World, Pope Alexander
VI divided the, as yet unknown, territory into two parts. Using
an imaginary 'line of demarcation', the land to the east of the
line, which ran north to south several hundred miles west of
the Azores and Cape Verdes, now belonged to Portugal, while
the land to the west was given to Spain. Almost forty years later
Francisco Pizarro set out for Peru to secure the pagan Kingdom
of the Incas for Charles V of Spain and the Catholic Church.

Pizarro was born circa 1476, the illegitimate son of Gonzola
Pizarro and Francisca González. His father was a Captain in the
Spanish military who had fought in the Neapolitan wars. There
is little reliable evidence about Pizarro's early life. He is
supposed to have been abandoned on the steps of the church of
Santa Maria in Trujillo, and there is even a story that he was
suckled by a cow. As a youth, Pizarro worked at herding pigs

and had no education other than that of a hard upbringing. It is probable that he remained illiterate throughout his life.

Francisco came from Estremadura, a region in Spain that produced an extraordinarily large number of men who went off to the New World to seek their fortunes and to glorify Spain. The conquistadors' lust for gold was infinite and their religious fervour genuine. Hernán Cortéz, the conqueror of the Aztecs, had been born in a nearby town, almost ten years after Pizarro.

In 1509, Pizarro joined the ill-fated Hojeda expedition that set off with the intention of colonizing the Panama Isthmus. It was to be a gruelling time for the inexperienced Pizarro. Left behind in charge of the new settlement of San Sebastian, Pizarro had to endure near starvation, disease and poisoned arrows from hostile natives, before the settlement had become so reduced in size that he had no choice but to flee. Using two tiny brigantine ships, Pizarro managed to cram the sixty surviving men on board. When one sank immediately he could do nothing but leave the men to their fate and sail away to Cartagena. Hojeda fared even worse. He was forced to beach his ship and walk more than 400 miles through jungle and swamps to reach the newly-founded settlement of Santo Domingo. Of the 1,250 men who left Spain on the expedition, only 200 survived and Hojeda died penniless.

But luck was on Pizarro's side. Upon arrival in Cartagena, he ran into Encisco, a business associate of Hojeda's who had arrived with a relief force of 150 men. They set sail towards Uraba, but Enciso managed to lose his ship on a sandbank. Control of the expedition would have passed to Pizarro, but the emergence of the adventurer, Vasco Núñez de Balboa, denied him this opportunity.

Pizarro joined Balboa on an expedition through Panama's jungles, and on 29 September 1513 they waded into the waters of the Pacific. It had been the first successful crossing of the Isthmus and was an incredible achievement. On the edges of the Mar del Sur, Pizarro first heard stories of a fabulous golden land to the south.

The news that Balboa had discovered a new ocean created a sensation in Spain, and gave new hope that a route through to the wealthy Spice Islands would soon be found. But the arrival of a new Governor in Panama, Pedrarias Dávila, soon dashed Balboa's dreams of pure exploration. Pedrarias, who had been appointed Governor due to his court connections, and Balboa hated each other on sight; the small town would not be big enough to hold them both. Within a few months, Pedrarias had Balboa arrested on charges of conspiracy. Pizarro, who arrested him, had finally got his revenge for being overlooked as the leader of the Uraba expedition. Balboa was executed.

Pizarro, a true opportunist, now quickly transferred his loyalty to Pedrarias who sent him to trade with the natives along the Pacific coast. When the capital was transferred to Panama he helped Pedrarias to subjugate the warlike tribes of Veraguas, and in 1520 he accompanied Espinosa on his expedition into the territory of Cacique Urraca, situated in the present Republic of Costa Rica.

By the age of forty-five Francisco Pizarro had little to show for his numerous expeditions. Accounts of the achievements of Hernán Cortéz, and the return of Pascuel de Andagoya from his expedition to the southern part of Panama, fired Pizarro with enthusiasm.

All the expeditions, prior to that of Andagoya, had been to the north up as far as Honduras. Few of the newly-arrived adventurers were sailors, and the land to the north and west offered safer prospects than the unknown perils of the great South Sea that stretched in unlimited vastness beyond the horizon.

In Panama, Pizarro formed a partnership with Diego de Almagro, a soldier of fortune, and Hernando de Luque, a Spanish cleric. Their plans were to form a company to conquer the lands to the south of Panama. Their project seemed so utterly unattainable that the people of Panama called them the 'company of lunatics'. But Pizarro had spent thirteen years in the Indies and he knew that the biggest prizes went to the boldest and to those who got there first. Luque, a schoolmaster and treasurer of the company's funds, provided the financial backing and with the consent of the governor they began fitting out two small boats for a voyage of discovery.

Pizarro embarked on 14 November 1524, accompanied by 112 Spaniards, a few horses, and a few Indian servants. He sailed his ship into the Bira River and then decided to continue overland. The going was treacherous, among swamps fringed with dense jungle and vast hills. Finally, Pizarro decided that travel by sea was the lesser of two evils and they returned to the ship. Once on board they were hit by calms, and the food and water began to run out. Faced with an increasingly hostile crew, Pizarro made the decision to allow those who wished to return to leave for Panama under the auspices of one of his captains, Montenegro.

It was over six weeks before Montenegro returned with provisions. In the meantime Pizarro and his men had been marooned in the swamps of Puerto de la Hambre (Port of Famine), where they had been reduced to eating shellfish and seaweed on the shore. But Pizarro had managed to make contact with the natives and listened to stories of a powerful kingdom to the south. He also had his first look at some gold ornaments and his appetite was whetted.

They headed south again, hugging the coast, but all they found were deserted villages, a little maize and more crude gold objects. In desperation, Pizarro marched inland, but was attacked by Indians in the foothills of the Cordilleras Mountains. It was a bloody engagement and Pizarro was wounded before they withdrew.

Pizarro and his crew had travelled only as far as Punta Quemada, on the coast of modern-day Columbia. Once back on board, they fled back to the Pearl Island archipelago in Panama. They finally met up with Almagro's ship at Chicama, and Pizarro discovered that Almagro had only made it a little further up the coast before being forced to return. However, the adventurers were not going to give up so easily. Almagro and Luque returned to Panama to meet with the governor. Pizarro, who hated bureaucracy, was extremely conscious of his lack of education and sent his treasurer, Nicholas de Rivera, to get money and supplies for a new expedition.

A second request to Pedrarias for permission to recruit volunteers for a new expedition was met with hostility. Their first voyage had lost money and Pedrarias was already organizing an expedition to Nicaragua. Their luck changed with the arrival of a new Governor, Don Pedro de los Rios, and the necessary funds were raised. Pizarro and Almagro were made joint leaders of the new expedition and on 10 March 1526, a contract was signed between Pizarro, Almagro and Luque. They agreed to split all conquered territory and any gold, silver and precious stones three ways, less the one-fifth required by Charles V, King of Spain.

They purchased two ships and Pizarro and Almagro directed their course to the mouth of the San Juan River. Pizarro set off with a group of soldiers to explore the mainland, capturing some Indians and collecting gold. Upon his return the two ships separated; Almagro went back to Panama to get re-enlistments and sell the gold; and the other ship, under the command of Ruiz, set sail for the south. Ruiz got as far as Punta de Pasados, half a degree south of the equator, and after making observations and collecting information, returned to Pizarro. Pizarro had ventured inland once more, but to no avail. All they had found was impenetrable rainforest and deep ravines, and had struggled back to the coast, near to starvation, to await the return of his partners. After seventy days, Ruiz returned with just the news they had been waiting for. He was full of tales of an increasingly populated, and friendly land, overflowing with riches. More importantly, he had two Peruvians on board to verify the stories.

Shortly after Almagro returned from Panama with eighty newly arrived recruits from Spain. With full bellies and more men, the two ships sailed on to Quito, the edge of the mighty Inca Empire. Set upon by hostile natives, the adventurers had no option but to retreat. After a bitter row, Pizarro agreed to remain behind whilst Almagro returned to Panama to sell the gold they had found, and drum up more reinforcements.

Pizarro camped on the island of Gallo, a barren, flat place. Living an unhappy existence on the desolate island, it was not long before Pizarro's men became mutinous. When Almagro's ship departed they sent a note, concealed in a bale of cotton, implying that Pizarro was holding them against their will.

When the note came to the governor's attention, any chance that Almagro had of maintaining the governor's support ended, and two ships were dispatched to bring Pizarro back.

When the ships reached Gallo they found the men in a state of near-starvation. Those that were left had been drenched by tropical rains, their clothes were in rags and their bodies, having been scorched by the sun, were covered in sores. Almagro and Luque had sent letters imploring Pizarro not to return nor give up all they had worked for and so Pizarro, in true conquistador fashion, decided to stay and ignore the governor's command. Drawing a line in the sand he summoned the remaining men saying, 'Gentlemen, this line represents toil, hunger, thirst, weariness, sickness and all other vicissitudes that our undertaking will involve. There lies Peru with all its riches; here, Panama and its poverty. Choose each man, what best becomes a brave Castilian. For my part I go to the South.' Then he stepped over the line – thirteen chose to remain with him, one of whom was his navigator, Ruiz.

The forlorn, abandoned men stood and watched as the two ships set sail for Panama and disappeared over the horizon. All was not lost, however, as Almago and Luque were able to persuade the governor to give them and Pizarro another chance. Reluctantly the governor agreed to back them and one ship, with no soldiers, was provided, with the stipulation that they had six months before they had to return. It had taken months to obtain consent from the governor, but Pizarro had learnt from previous experience and during this time had organized the building of rafts and relocated to the island of Gorgona, seventy-five miles up the coast. This beautiful island was stocked with fresh water and virgin forests, and by the time the governor's ship found them Pizarro and his followers were in good spirits.

Leaving Gorgona behind the ship now sailed south, crossed the equator, and arrived in the Bay of Tumbes. On the land they could see towers and temples rising above the green fields. They had arrived in the Empire of the Incas.

The following morning a fleet of rafts with Inca warriors came out to investigate the mysterious new arrivals. Pizarro invited them on board and asked his two Peruvian crew members to show them around. One of the Inca soldiers was a member of the government and he invited Pizarro to visit the city. He returned from the city with tales of a temple tapestried with plates of gold and silver, and information on the city's defences. With only a small number of men, Pizarro was unable to take what he wanted, but vowed to return later on.

For now, however, it was time to turn back, time to raise an army, to shed the cloak of discoverer, and assume the armour of conqueror.

Tales of the Sun God King would be enough to set Panama ablaze with excitement, or so Pizarro believed. On his return, after eighteen months away, Pizarro was fêted; everyone marvelled at his achievements, but the full-scale expedition that he was proposing was deemed beyond the colony's capacity. The governor was not a conquistador so Luque proposed that they petition the Crown of Spain direct and Pizarro, full of his new-found confidence, left for Spain.

Immediately Pizarro arrived, he was jailed as punishment for an old debt, but fortunately, tales of his exploits had reached the court, and hungry for more money from the New World, Pizarro was released. He was brought to Toledo to meet with Charles V, and after securing the King's blessing Pizarro now had to deal with the Council of the Indies – a bureaucratic machine that had grown fat on the exploits of others.

Finally, on 26 July 1529, Queen Joanna The Mad agreed to Pizarro's terms. He was made Governor, Captain-General for life and granted a large salary. Luque was made Bishop of Tumbes as well as 'Protector' of all the natives in Peru, and Ruiz became Grand Pilot of the Southern Ocean with a salary to match. Almagro got virtually nothing; Pizarro had betrayed him on the premise that Almagro had not been present on the voyage of discovery.

But Pizarro's troubles were far from over. Although the crown had granted him a title they expected the expedition to be self-financing and money still had to be found. Spain might reap the rewards, but they were not prepared to take a risk financially. Elated by his success, however, Pizarro returned to his home in

Trujillo to get more men. His brothers Gonzalo, Juan and Hernando joined him on the adventure. Hernando, a terribly cruel man, was to become Pizarro's right-hand man. It took a further six months to raise the money and fit out the ships. Finally they left for Panama in January 1531 and sailed to Nombre De Dios to meet with Almagro. On arrival Pizarro clashed with Almagro immediately, not helped by Hernando who was openly scornful of the old man. Eventually peace was restored, but from the start the three chief personalities were at odds.

With extraordinary arrogance and pride, the fifty-five-year-old Pizarro was now embarking on his voyage of conquest. He had three vessels, two large and one small, 180 men, 27 horses, arms, ammunition and stores. With these supplies he intended to conquer an empire that stretched 2,000 miles south from Cabo Blanco, included one of the world's greatest mountain chains and extended inland to the rainforests of the Amazon.

Initially the forces of nature halted the invaders in San Mateo Bay, 350 miles away from Tumbes. Pizarro then decided to put his men on shore and march them south. His men looted and sacked a small, undefended town. It was the height of stupidity, because for just a small immediate financial gain, Pizarro had lost not only any hope of achieving surprise, but also the goodwill of the natives. Incarcerated in their quilted cotton clothing and heavy armour, his men became victims of the tortuous heat, and many died. It was the most senseless start to a campaign that any general could have conceived.

Eventually they arrived at the island of Puna, having been joined by two more ships carrying the Royal Treasurer and administration officials. Pizarro then started a war between the Puna and the Tumbes (the Puna's mortal enemies), and the Spanish were forced to seek refuge in the forest. Evacuation became a necessity and with the arrival of more volunteers and horses, Pizarro decided to return to Tumbes on the mainland. But Tumbes was now almost a shell. Initially furious and disheartened, Pizarro ranted and raved. But his phenomenal luck had not deserted him. Unbeknown to the Spanish they had chosen the ideal time for an invasion of Peru. The Inca Empire was in the middle of a bloody civil war.

The empire had been in existence since 1250 when the first Inca, Mando Copa, had made Cuzco his capital and begun expanding his empire. By 1493, just thirty years before Pizarro's arrival, they had conquered the whole of Peru, parts of Bolivia and Equador and most of Chile – an area of about 380,000 square miles. The Inca armies contained a total of 300,000 troops.

Huayna Capac, the Sun God, had died in 1524 and faced with ill omens and a vast area to control, he decided to split the Empire between his two sons, Huascar and Atahulpa. Atahulpa was given control of the north, while Huascar was given the area centred round Cuzco. The year of Huayna Capac's death was the year that Pizarro had first landed in Tumbes. Five years after Huayna's death Atahulpa marched against his brother. In a ruthless and bloody campaign Atahulpa had laid waste to entire provinces, and in the final battle near Cuzco he captured Huascar.

Pizarro knew that now he had the chance to go for the total conquest of the vast Inca nation. With this knowledge his whole attitude changed. He set off into the interior with a small force to win over the local population and to turn his men into a disciplined fighting machine. Any Indian chiefs who opposed him were burnt and soon the whole region was pacified.

Pizarro now had 110 foot soldiers and 67 horse troops, of which only 20 were armed. Should he march now or wait for reinforcements? He pondered his dilemma, well aware that Atahulpa had in excess of 40,000 warriors at his command. Finally in September, Pizarro marched. By mid-November his tiny force was descending the Andes into Cajamarca where Atahulpa, waiting with his tented army by the hot springs, meditated on his course of action.

Atahulpa had been aware of the Spanish progress right from the start, but was unsure what to make of the visitors to his kingdom. It is highly unlikely that he felt any sense of foreboding, surrounded as he was by his vast army. He had only to speak and whatever he commanded would be done. However, he was consumed with curiosity. He had received reports of the Spanish ships, their guns and firearms and how the Spanish rode animals much larger than the Peruvian llama. So he waited with his army, letting the Spanish approach him unmolested, even giving them the stone-built security of Cajamarca for a rest camp.

Once in the relative safety of Cajamarca, Pizarro waited for Atahulpa to respond. Finally, he sent a delegation of twenty horsemen to arrange a meeting. It was doubtless a daunting sight for Pizarro's small band of adventurers as they rode into the heart of a great conquering army. Atahulpa greeted them wearing a collar of large emeralds; his whole cavalcade blazing with gold. The Spanish caballeros in their armour also made a deep impression and Atahulpa agreed to meet with Pizarro the following day. He set off armed to the hilt with warriors lining the route and when he was within a short distance of the town, stopped and sent a message to Pizarro saying he would arrive the next morning.

Meanwhile tensions were building in the Spanish camp and Pizarro devised a plan. He wrote to Atahulpa implying that the Inca king lacked the necessary courage of true nobility. Atahulpa's two most trusted generals, Quizquiz and Challcuchima were fighting in Cuzco, and in his desire to demonstrate his bravery Atahulpa set off to meet Pizarro's force with only 6,000 unarmed warriors.

When he came before Pizarro, a Dominican friar named Valverde thrust a Bible into Atahulpa's hand and urged him to renounce his own divinity in favour of Jesus and acknowledge the Emperor Charles V as a king greater than himself. Atahulpa exploded with anger and threw the Bible to the ground. Pizarro gave the signal, and with the battle-cry, Santiago! the guns and cannon boomed out across the square. Spanish troops attacked, their swords flashing in the afternoon sun. The Peruvians died fighting with their bare hands in defence of Atahulpa. The attendants and some of the unarmed Incas broke down a wall and fled into the countryside, pursued by the cavalry. The butchery of those that remained trapped in the square did not stop until it was almost dark. Such was the blood lust of the Spaniards that it was only the intervention of Pizarro himself that saved the Inca king, who was imprisoned immediately.

By capturing the Sun God, Pizarro had virtually immobilized the entire Inca army. The soldiers eventually melted away into the surrounding countryside and no attempt was made to rescue Atahulpa. In the baths the Spanish found 5,000 women who they promptly defiled. Then came the looting. One gold vase weighed over 100 kilograms. It was unbelievable. Pizarro suddenly found the great empire wide open and it had all been achieved by a stroke in which not a single Spaniard lost his life. Indeed, none had even been wounded, except for Pizarro himself who had received a sword cut whilst defending Atahulpa.

Mysteriously Atahulpa made no attempts to contact his generals, and when he saw the Spanish lust for gold, he made Pizarro an offer he couldn't refuse. He proposed that, in exchange for his freedom, one of the immense halls in Cajamarca be filled with gold, but to make sure that the terms of ransom would never be met, Pizarro insisted that another room be filled twice over with silver. Atahulpa had bought time and probably still believed that he could escape, but did not seem to doubt Pizarro's word of honour.

As several weeks passed, tension mounted in the Spanish camp, before the treasure started to trickle in. The carriers had vast distances to surmount and the treasure pile grew slowly. Irate at the time it was taking Pizarro dispatched three of his men to oversee the dismantling of the great Temple of the Sun. The men were treated like gods but behaved appallingly, even ravishing the sacred Inca Virgins of the Sun.

Rumours abounded in Cajamarca of an attack and Pizarro sent his brother, Hernando and some men to investigate. By February 1533 Pizarro was joined by Almagro and reinforcements. Pizarro wanted to move on, but had to wait for the arrival of tribes who were hostile to Atahulpa.

By now the treasure amassed stood at 1,326,539 gold pesos and the rooms were still not filled. Pizarro decided that he had waited long enough and that the spoils should be divided. Hernando was dispatched to Spain to report to the Emperor and give him his share.

Meanwhile the mood of the camp was rapidly building up

to the point where the men themselves would demand what Pizarro wanted most – to be rid of Atahulpa. The Inca king had now become an encumbrance. He had served his purpose. Pizarro had the gold: now he wanted power. An empire was within his grasp, but as long as the Inca king lived he provided a rallying point for resistance. His death had become a political and tactical necessity.

In order to make Atahulpa's death appear just and legal, Pizarro set up a court, with himself and Almagro as the judges, and proceeded to try the defeated warrior. Atahulpa was accused of twelve crimes including adultery, because he had many wives, and worshipping idols. Pizarro had turned Inquisitor in his new Empire.

The trial was a farce and Atahulpa was sentenced to be burnt to death. On 16 July 1533 he was carried by torchlight and placed on the stake.

Now the Spaniards were free to march on the capital, Cuzco. Throughout the months they had stayed at Cajamarca they had been living off the accumulated wealth of the Indians, slaughtering around 150 llamas a day, plundering the supplies, and demanding and receiving a steady supply of food from local chiefs. They were men without thought to the future and now they embarked on the destruction of the whole civilization.

On 15 November 1533, one year after arriving in Cajamarca, the Spanish entered the capital. On the march the Spanish had collected a further half-a-million gold pesos of treasure. Pizarro was now joined by other Spanish troops anxious to share in the wealth of the conquered Inca empire.

He was now absolute master of Peru – and would remain so for eight years. Had he had any real administrative ability, he could have had the co-operation of the whole nation. The Peruvians were a stoic race, accustomed to passive subservience. But Pizarro and his soldiers mistook passivity for cowardice, and they indulged in the worst excesses towards the population.

By 1535 the country appeared calmer and Pizarro left for the coast to found his new capital, Lima. Meanwhile, Almagro was governing Cuzco, having been made independent of Pizarro by the Emperor Charles. Unfortunately, in dividing up their areas of control, Charles had been extremely vague and both Pizarro and Almagro claimed Cuzco for their own. The city was split into factions and by the summer the Indians had finally reached breaking point. They were led by the young Inca, Manco, a son of Huayna Capac.

In a six-month siege most of the city was destroyed. Pizarro had made repeated attempts to relieve the garrison, but had failed. By now the whole country was in revolt against the senseless brutality of its foreign masters, and the Spanish only managed to hold on at the fortress of Sacahuaman. By August, the revolt had ended. Manco's supplies had run out and he was reduced to fighting a guerrilla war, moving from one fortress to another.

Pizarro attempted to meet with him but it was doomed to failure. When one of his messengers was killed, Pizarro had one of Manco's young wives captured, bound naked to a tree in front of his army, beaten half to death and then shot full of arrows. Such brutal actions would never lead to settlement between the two sides.

But Pizarro still had to deal with the conflict between Hernando and his old ally Almagro and he now dealt a fatal blow to his partner in one of the dirtiest double crosses of the conquest. Pretending that Hernando had been dispatched to Spain, Pizarro gathered his forces and defeated Almagro at the Battle of Las Salinas. Over 150 Spanish died and Almagro was captured and executed by Hernando.

Pizarro now settled down to administering his great kingdom and organized a series of expeditions to discover new lands, but while his brother Gonzalo was staggering out of the steaming forests of the Amazon, the fortunes of the Pizarro family were reaching their inevitable climax.

Discontent was rife throughout the country. More and more Spanish were flooding in every week and a band of discontented followers of Almagro's son swore revenge on Pizarro. On 26 June 1541, Pizarro was told of a plot against him, but he took little notice of it. Around midday the conspirators entered the Governor's palace and slew Pizarro, plunging their swords repeatedly into his body.

Francisco Pizarro, the peasant's son from Spain, was dead and with his death the age of the conquistadors was drawing to a close. In just over half a century a whole new world had been opened up. But the conquistadors were fighting men – the consolidation of the empire they had won was left to others. The once mighty Inca Empire was soon flooded with swarms of officials, but the new laws came too late to save the Indians.

IVAN IV, 'THE TERRIBLE'

TSAR OF ALL THE RUSSIAS

All the Russian sovereigns are autocrats and no one can find fault with them, the monarch can exercise his will over the slaves whom God has given him...If you do not obey the sovereign when he commits an injustice, not only do you become guilty of felony but you damn your soul, for God himself orders you to obey your prince blindly.

IVAN IV, LETTER TO PRINCE ANDREW KURBSKII

Even before Ivan's birth, the Patriarch of Jerusalem had predicted that his father, Vasily III, would have 'an evil son'. Just after his birth in the middle of a violent thunderstorm another prophecy foretold that, 'a tsar is born among you: two teeth has he. With one he will devour us; but with the other – you'. By the time of his death, fifty-four years later, Ivan IV well deserved his name of Grozny or Terrible. He had ordered and participated in the ruthless extermination of thousands of people; devoted associates and sworn enemies alike died amid hideous tortures. Villages, towns and an entire city perished. Ivan's tumultuous rages knew no bounds and he even killed his adored son in a fit of rage. The first Tsar of all the Russias, he had absolute power over millions of lives. Lacking any compassion for his subjects, he tortured, robbed or raped them purely for his own amusement.

Ivan was just three years old when the great bell of the Kremlin tolled for the death of his father. The Russian court was plunged into violence as Elena Glinskaya, his Catholic mother, fought to hold on to power, imprisoning and killing those who stood in her way. The regents, named by his father on his deathbed, were jealous and greedy for power. Intrigues and plots ruled the day. Outwardly, Ivan was treated well, but only when he was in the public eye. The regents tortured and killed people in front of the young impressionable Ivan, and nobles, sobbing in terror and fleeing from imminent death, kept him awake at night.

In this forbidding climate of spying, poisoning and violence, Ivan came to view life as might a predatory animal, eager to pursue his prey and enjoy its suffering. He took his frustration out on defenceless creatures such as dogs and cats when, after piercing their eyes and dropping them from the high towers of the Kremlin, he would run down the stairs to watch them die a slow death. It was more than an amusement; it was an apprenticeship.

Ignored by his mother, the seven-year-old became isolated and paranoid. His beloved nurse, Agrafena Obolensky, was sent to a convent by regent Prince Vasily Shuisky and Ivan and his younger brother, Yuri the idiot, became little more than beggars in the Kremlin. Armed men roamed the palace, frequently bursting into the Grand Prince's room, shoving him aside and taking whatever they pleased.

In 1538 Ivan watched as his mother died in agony; poisoned with mercury by the boyars, members of the landed nobility who ranked just below the princes. The boyars also had one of Ivan's few loyal confidants, Fydor Mishurin, skinned alive and left on public view in a Moscow square. For the rest of his childhood Ivan lived amid terror and brutality as rival families fought for power. It was to have a devastating effect on his sanity, and on his attitude towards the nation as a whole.

At the age of thirteen Ivan graduated from torturing animals to killing people. Just after Christmas, Ivan invited the boyars to a banquet and they watched in amazement as Ivan stood up and loudly accused them of taking advantage of his youth to further their own interests. He declared that he held everyone responsible, but would be satisfied with the blood of their leader, Prince Andrew Shuisky. Stunned, the boyars listened without objection. Instantly, Ivan's guards moved forward to seize the prince. He was thrown into an enclosure with a pack of starved hunting dogs and savaged to death. With Shuisky dead, the boyars conceded that their rule had ended, and that Ivan had complete power.

Ivan was by now a very disturbed young man as well as a

voracious drinker. He roamed the Moscow streets with a gang of thugs, drinking, stealing from people and raping women. He often disposed of victims by having them hanged, strangled, buried alive or thrown to the bears. But Ivan never lost the notion of his exceptional dignity. When he became drunk, when he fornicated, it was God who was getting drunk and fornicating, through him. He believed that God was saving him for a special purpose. Ironically he became increasingly devout, believing that the church would support his views and that he was God's representative on earth, but even his way of worshipping was violent. As he kneeled in front of the altar he would throw himself down before religious icons, banging his head so hard against the floor that he developed a callus. It was a habit that was to remain with him throughout his life.

By the age of sixteen Ivan had become a volatile young man, but one ready to assume the role for which he had been born. The Russian people, dominated by the boyars, tried appealing to their young sovereign, but Ivan refused to be troubled by external events. One day, while out hunting near Novgorod, he was approached by fifty councillors with a petition complaining of the oppressive measures that afflicted them. Ivan refused to listen and, illogically believing an attempt had been made on his life, he had the petitioners decapitated. One of the victims had been his childhood friend, Fydor Vorontzov. Ivan now believed that his justice was infallible and his power sacred.

Tall and thin, hawk-nosed, his face lengthened by a reddish brown beard, and with bright blue piercing eyes, Ivan stood before all the boyars and court in the vast throne room and announced his own succession, and in a significant break with tradition he demanded his own title – Tsar of all the Russias. At a stroke Ivan had distanced himself from the princes and boyars in Moscow and placed himself above all other European heads of state. He even had a hastily prepared genealogy made up to prove that he was the direct descendent of the Roman Emperor Augustus.

Not long after this Ivan chose his first wife, Anastasia Romanovna, in the traditional ceremony of smotriny, when all the young, virginal princesses and daughters of noblemen were presented to him. Although Ivan had initially wanted to make a marriage alliance with a European court, the union was a happy one, for Ivan and for Russia. His new Tsarina was to keep some of Ivan's cruelty under control. He called her his 'little heifer' – finally Ivan had someone to love. They married in February 1547 and were to have thirteen years of happy marriage. The silent, strong Anastasia bore him six children, two of whom survived infancy.

Within months of both his marriage and accession, however, Ivan had a new problem to face. Moscow, a city largely constructed from wood, was slowly being consumed by fire. Thousands died and were made homeless, but to Ivan, steeped in his own importance, the disaster could mean only one thing: God had singled him out for personal punishment. His belief was confirmed by a a priest called Sylvester, who told him that the fires were God's punishment for his sins, and Sylvester urged Ivan to purify his soul. Having always thought that he and God were friends, Ivan decided on a huge act of public penance and in a cynical move that was to become a pattern of his reign, he also made use of the opportunity to strengthen his regal position.

Up until now it had been the Glinsksys that had maintained control over Russia. Loaded with honours and riches, they oppressed the people, extorted money and ruthlessly meted out punishment to those who dared to complain. They were hated by the common people and viewed by most of the boyars as symbols of tyranny, dishonesty and vice. In a packed Red Square, Ivan, draped in gold and spangled with jewels, prostrated himself before his people apologizing for the behaviour of the boyars and promising to act as the peoples' protector, urging them to be united by love. He claimed that his soul had been seized by terror and his spirit subdued when pity entered his heart. The Glinsksy family fled for their lives.

Shortly after this speech, Ivan began reforming the government. He created a new type of council, the Izbrannaya Rada or Chosen Council, composed of members of the nobility and clergy who were known for their wisdom, sober judgement and devotion. The assembly was dominated by two men; the Metropolitan of Moscow, Macarius, the most cultivated man in Russia; and Sylvester, the mystical preacher who dared to speak to the Tsar as a simple penitent. Ivan then embarked on a massive overhauling of the State, the Church and the Army, creating an elite force called the Streltsi. He demanded that all territories under his control should adhere to the same laws, and condemned corruption. Ivan was obsessed with the idea of unifying his country and taking judicial, administrative and fiscal powers away from the local nobility.

Ivan also imperiously demanded that Russia start trading directly with England, and he created trading links with Sweden and Holland. Domestic success was coupled with significant military victories on Russia's southern and eastern borders, but Ivan had three causes for concern: the Swedes, the Poles and the Tartars. Using the Streltsi, who were equipped in European style, and given wages and uniforms, he first captured the city of Kazan, stronghold of the Tartars, and by 1554 his victories had added nearly one million square kilometres to the realm. It was during the campaign against the Tartars that Ivan first became known under the title Grozny, although initially it was given to reflect his qualities as a mighty ruler, rather than his role as an instigator of terror.

But Ivan's penchant for sadism and revenge was never far from the surface. In March 1553 he fell dangerously ill and subsequently demanded that the boyars swear allegiance to his one-year-old son, Dimitri. Initially they refused, fearing that if the Tsar died, it would mean anarchy and a return to the rule of the regents. Furious at their disloyalty, all Ivan's old hatreds resurfaced, but bound by an oath he had made to God to forgive the schemers if he should recover, Ivan coldly bided his time. Ironically, just after Ivan's recovery, the royal couple was visiting a monastery to give thanks to God for his revival, when a nurse dropped Dimitri into the river and the baby drowned. Nine months later Anastasia gave birth to another son, Ivan.

For thirteen years, thanks to the advice of his wife, alongside Sylvester, and Alexei Adashev, (the Chamberlain) Ivan had governed the country with relative wisdom. Even foreign observers had acknowledged he was an outstanding sovereign. However, on 7 August 1560, Ivan's beloved Anastasia died after a lingering, painful illness. The people of Moscow wept for their charitable Tsarina, their lamentations drowning out the priests' chanting. Ivan walked, bare-headed behind the coffin, supported by his brother and afterwards haunted the empty rooms his wife had left behind, ranting and screaming in desperation. Once more isolated and trying to comprehend the reasons for this punishment, Ivan became convinced that Anastasia had been poisoned and suddenly all his old cruelty resurfaced. The God that had taken away Anastasia was cruel and irrational – from now on he would behave the same way. Like God, he was now exempt from all moral laws, and since God had offended him, he had the right to offend God.

Ivan raged against the boyars as he banged his head on the floor, in full view of the court, and began to smash up the furniture. His suspicion then descended into paranoia and he had whole families obliterated. From every side informers flocked into the Kremlin, eagerly pandering to Ivan. To oblige their Tsar, judges no longer required any genuine evidence, and many of the nobility, who had fought loyally in the Tsar's wars, were tortured and strangled alongside their children. He had Sylvester exiled to a monastery, where he died in obscurity and Adashev imprisoned where he died two months later in mysterious circumstances.

Henceforth, Ivan's married life would be unstable, underlining his egocentricity, insecurity and manic temperament. In 1561, he married a Circassian beauty, Maria Temriukovna, but he soon tired of her. She died in 1569 and he married Martha Sobakin, a merchant's daughter, but she died two weeks later. Ivan's fourth wife was Anna Koltovskaya, whom he sent to a convent in 1575. He married a fifth time to Anna Wassilchikura, who was soon replaced by Wassilissa Melentiewna. She foolishly took a lover, who was impaled under her window before she, too, was dispatched to a convent. After his seventh wedding day, Ivan discovered that his new bride, Maria Dolgurukaya, was not a virgin. He had her drowned the next day. His last wife, Maria Nagaya, whom he married in 1581, outlived him.

The prisons and monasteries of Russia now overflowed with Ivan's victims. The harder he struck, the more he wanted to strike, and the blood that was shed, far from quenching his thirst, whetted his appetite for fresh excesses. To replace the boyars who were guilty of having displeased him, Ivan chose men of the petty nobility, men who never contradicted him and who encouraged him in his debauchery. Over the next year Ivan was to lose his brother Yuri, his youngest son Vasily and Metropolitan Macarius. Ivan's last links with the past had gone – there was no one left whom he felt he could trust.

Shortly before Christmas in 1564, Ivan suddenly packed his belongings and treasures and secretly left Moscow for Aleksandrovskaia Sloboda with his family, announcing his intention to abdicate. It was an absurd notion, because, for sixteenth-century Russians, he was not just considered the Head of State, but the State itself. However, it was a brilliant stroke of manipulation. Ivan wrote two letters, the first listed the disorders, betrayals and crimes of the nobility and generals, accusing them of looting the treasury and mistreating the peasants. The second letter, addressed to the foreign and Russian merchants and all the Christian people of Moscow, told how he loved them as much as he hated the boyars and churchmen. The letters were broadcast and Russia was thrown into confusion, the populace pleaded for his return and a delegation of senior clergy and nobility was sent to the Tsar to beg him to reconsider. His gamble had paid off, and after a month Ivan returned victoriously to Moscow, but not before he had demanded, and received, absolute power to punish anyone he considered disloyal, and the ability to dispose of their estates. Henceforth he would be the sole interpreter and executor of the will of God, with authority above and beyond the Church. The reign of terror was about to begin.

On 2 February 1565, Ivan re-entered Moscow. According to witnesses, the thirty-four-year-old Tsar had the appearance of an old man. His face was grey and wrinkled, his eyes were dull, his hair scant, his lips thin and clenched and his forehead deeply furrowed. Within a month of his return, Ivan had divided Russia in half. The Zemshchina, which would be under Ivan's power, would keep its Duma, or parliament of boyars and functionaries; and the Oprichnina, the richest part, would be the Tsar's private domain, which he would administer as he pleased. On 4 February, the very day the Oprichnina was established, the executions began.

To help him instigate his absolute rule of evil, Ivan created the Oprichniki, Russia's first Secret Police. The mere sight of the Oprichniki instilled fear. They rode through the streets of Moscow and into the countryside dressed in black, riding black horses, carrying brooms and dogs' heads as symbols of their mission to sweep away treachery and then gnaw it to death. Ivan was establishing a new nobility of paid servants. Among the Oprichniki all that counted was a devotion to satisfy Ivan's desires. Many were vicious criminals. They were above the law and to insult them was a crime punishable by death. They could impose fines, torture, rape, pillage and burn without any fear of reprisal.

The boyars now realized that by confiscating their villages, peasants and property, Ivan meant to break their power permanently. It is estimated that as many as 10,000 members of the nobility died at the hands of the Oprichniki, and 12,000 families were forcibly relocated and their lands seized.

The more Ivan oppressed the country, the more he felt he was hated; the more he felt hated, the more determined he was to discover who was plotting against his life. Anxiety prevented him from sleeping and he saw evil omens everywhere. Moscow no longer seemed safe, and so it was that Ivan moved back to Aleksandrovskaia Sloboda, to a palace surrounded by moats and ramparts. The interior of the sinister palace reflected the four different aspects of Ivan's personality. Some of the rooms were superbly decorated; others were crammed with precious books and parchments; still others resembled monastic cells. The rooms underground were divided into a series of dungeons.

Delirious with fervent piety, Ivan handpicked the most aggressive 300 Oprichniki and installed them in the palace, which he transformed into a monastery. The men, he announced, would be his monks, and he would be their abbot. Each brother wore a black cassock over his gold-embroidered coat trimmed with fur. Ivan sincerely believed he had created a new monastic order.

Following a rigid timetable including a four-hour service followed by lunch and a short nap, Ivan and his men would visit the dungeons. They regularly performed sacrilegious masses that were followed by extended orgies of rape and torture. Ivan supervised as ribs were torn out of men's chests with sharp and hissing hot pincers. Drunken licentiousness was alternated with passionate acts of repentance. After throwing himself down before the altar with such vehemence that his forehead would be bloody, Ivan would rise and read sermons on the Christian virtues to his drunken retainers. Banquets would follow the sermons and entertainments would be laid on to amuse Ivan. Maliuta-Skuratov, one of the most cruel of the brotherhood, would force naked peasant girls to chase after hens while the Oprichniki fired arrows at them. After a short sleep Ivan would return to the church to pray. Lifting up his soul he would hear God whispering in his ear the names of new victims. On his knees, between prayers, he would give his bloodiest orders.

By the age of thirty-four, Ivan had become a figure of fear. He often carried a long wooden staff, the steel-pointed end of which he used to maim or kill. He would lash out at people who offended him. Prince Boris Telupa was, 'drawn upon a long sharp-made stake, which entered the lower part of his body and came out of his neck; upon which he survived for 15 hours, talking to his mother who had been brought to behold the sight. After her son's death she was given to 100 gunners, who defiled her to death, and the Tsar's hungry hounds then devoured her flesh and bones.' No one was immune to Ivan's evil – his treasurer, Nikita Funikov, was boiled to death in a cauldron. In fact Ivan's delusions were so extreme that in 1567 he applied to Elizabeth I for political asylum whilst at the same time offering himself as her suitor.

Around the Tsar there was nothing but weakness and

cowardice. He was being advised by men like Bomelius, a Dutch adventurer, who claimed to be a doctor of magical sciences and who further fanned the flames of Ivan's paranoia by reminding him how many enemies he still had.

Few were prepared to challenge Ivan's rule. In 1568, when Metropolitan Philip, the head of the Russian Orthodox Church, begged for mercy on behalf of men unjustly accused of rebellion, Ivan did not initially dare to attack him directly. Instead, he contented himself with having a few clergy arrested and tortured. A few months later, however, when Philip ill-advisedly reprimanded Ivan for allowing an Oprichnik to wear a skullcap while celebrating mass, Ivan's patience snapped and he had him arrested. Languishing in prison, Philip failed to bless the Novgorod expedition, where up to 60,000 citizens of the city were massacred, and he was strangled by Ivan's faithful henchman, Maliuta-Skuratov.

Novgorod suffered when Ivan decided he was no longer satisfied with punishing individuals; he had to punish whole towns. For a long time he had been irritated by the presumption of Novgorod, a town that had only recently been united to the crown. Initially content with taking over 650 hostages back to Moscow, a subversive letter, forged by a criminal with a grievance against the town and 'signed' by all the notables of the city, gave Ivan the excuse he needed. In December 1569, Ivan left Moscow at the head of an army of his Oprichniki. Accompanied by his son, Ivan, who shared his father's taste for crude pleasures and blood, Ivan amused himself on the journey by ordering the massacre of the inhabitants of Klim. He then prayed in a monastery for five days while the Oprichniki went from house to house, torturing whomever they pleased.

Then, on 8 January 1570, Ivan entered the terrified, deserted city of Novgorod. First he sacked and looted the cathedral and the next day he set about dispensing justice. A German mercenary wrote that, '…the Czar mounted a horse and brandished his spear and charged in and ran people through while his son watched the entertainment.' Every day for five weeks a thousand citizens were brought into the main square where they were systematically tortured and slaughtered. The Oprichniki flogged their victims, broke their limbs, cut out their tongues, slit their nostrils, castrated them and roasted them over slow fires. Then they were flung into the icy waters of the River Volkhov, whole families at a time. Those who rose to the surface were dispatched with boat hooks, lances and axes by the Oprichniki in boats. So many bodies clogged the Volkhov, that it overflowed its banks. Finally, on 12 February, Ivan had one survivor from each street brought to him. Expecting death, they saw that Ivan wore a kindly expression. He had emerged from the bloodbath refreshed and rejuvenated. He told them to go home in peace. The decimation of Novgorod was over, but the city would never recover.

Later the same year, the terror reached a fever pitch in Moscow as Ivan instigated mass trials. Ivan watched from his balcony as workmen set up seventeen gallows, an enormous cauldron of water suspended over a vast pile of wood, a frying pan as big as a man, and ropes stretched taut to saw bodies in two by friction. Over 300 people were hanged, boiled or hacked to death in front of St Basil's Cathedral in Red Square, which had been built in celebration of Ivan's military victories.

On the morning of 24 May 1571, the Tartars invaded Moscow, setting fire to houses on the outskirts. A high wind spread the blaze. The citizens tried to find safety in the Kremlin, but the gates had been barricaded and many were crushed to death in the panic. In less than three hours, Moscow was reduced to a smoking ruin. Only the Kremlin, surrounded by its high walls, remained intact. The Tsar fled to Aleksandrovskaia Sloboda. In 1572 the Tartars returned again to Moscow, but fortunately for Ivan, Prince Vorotynsky, with a massively outnumbered force, won a resounding victory. Although he had nothing whatever to do with the victory, Ivan took all the credit, returning to Moscow triumphant. Six years later, Ivan personally tortured Vorotynsky to death. He had become a national hero, something Ivan could not tolerate.

The strength of Ivan's army now gave him security and, deciding that the Oprichniki were a blot on his image abroad, he dissolved them. This led to even more chaos as the chain of command broke down. The Oprichniki and Ivan had led the country to catastrophe by ravaging almost all the land under its control. Great stretches of countryside remained uncultivated and famine and plague arrived in Russia.

By 1578 Ivan was in great physical pain. He had developed large saline deposits on his backbone and the slightest movement would cause him agony. He could not wear himself out with fasting and prayer and the physical exhaustion made it impossible for him to kneel or bow down.

Ivan's rages were now fuelled by physical torment. On 9 November 1582, he assaulted his daughter-in-law because he did not like the dress she was wearing, causing her to miscarry. Ivan, the son and heir, quarrelled with his father and in the heat of the argument Ivan struck his son on the head with his wooden staff. He died a few days later. Fydor, the new heir, was a dwarf with a huge head and nose, who was both incompetent and childless. Ivan's power, limited by nothing and no one, would have to pass into the hands of a nobody.

Knocking his head against his son's coffin and making animal noises, Ivan was consumed with guilt and fear and demented by paranoia; he now became addicted to the ingestion of mercury, which he kept bubbling in a cauldron in his rooms. Fearing God's wrath, Ivan stopped all executions, repented for what he had done, and asked God to forgive him. One year later he gathered his sons together and warned them to be merciful rulers and think before casting people into disgrace. He asked for special lists to be made for prayers for those wrongly killed and sent money for their souls to be prayed for.

Ivan's years of debauchery had left its mark. He had long looked older than his years with long white hair dangling from a bald pate on to his shoulders, but towards the end he was grossly overweight and had to be carried on a litter. His body swelled, his skin peeled and, 'he began to swell grievously in his cods, with which he had most horribly offended above fifty years, boasting of a thousand virgins deflowered and thousands of children of his begetting destroyed.'

Just before his death the Tsar summoned sixty soothsayers

who told fortunes by the stars and they told him he would die on 18 March 1584. That day, Ivan went through his will, just in case, but he felt well, despite the gloomy predictions. He sent his adviser Belsky to warn the soothsayers that they would either be burnt or buried alive for their obvious lying. But the soothsayers were adamant. 'The day will end only when the sun goes down' was their reply. Having taken a bath, the Tsar settled down to play chess and dropped dead. An Englishman, who happened to be present, Jerome Gorsay, wrote that the Tsar was 'asphyxiated'. Other contemporaries, agreeing that his death was violent, suggested that he was poisoned, but it is unlikely that we will ever know what really happened. An analysis of his skeleton found no traces of violence, but then he was so weakened by illness that he could easily have been smothered.

Ivan left behind a joyless Russia. The chaos in which the administration was in, the bitter resentment of the boyars who had survived his purges, the foreign enemies whose hatred that Ivan's campaigns of pillage, torture and desolation had sharpened – all compounded to leave the country weak and divided. Countless acres of cultivated land had been abandoned by farmers during the terror of the Oprichniki, and forests had begun reclaiming the land.

During his reign of darkness hardly a family of noble birth was left whole, and some had been completely eliminated. Through his campaign of terror Ivan, Tsar of all the Russias, had created a system in which people who learned to hold their tongue, who not only never allowed themselves to speak their mind, but also did not even try to have an opinion, survived. He had laid the foundation for the top-heavy, unpredictable, often tyrannical autocracy of Tsarism – foundations that would eventually lead to its demise.

RASPUTIN

THE 'MAD MONK' WHO BROUGHT DOWN A DYNASTY

*Understanding Rasputin is the key to understanding both the
soul and the brutality of the Russia that came after him. He
was a precursor of the millions of peasants who, with religious
consciousness in their souls, would nevertheless tear down
churches and who, with a dream of the reign of Love and
Justice, would murder, rape and flood the country with blood,
in the end destroying themselves.*

EDVARD RADZINSKY

In December 1916, the bloated, castrated body of a man was
dragged from the freezing waters of the River Neva in St
Petersburg. As news of his identity leaked out, headlines in
Russian newspapers screamed, 'GRIGORI RASPUTIN HAS
CEASED TO EXIST!' People from all walks of life, both rich and
poor, celebrated the death of the 'mad monk' who had become
perhaps the most hated man in Russia. Implicated in murder,
corruption and extortion, Rasputin was instrumental in wiping
out the 300-year-old Romanov dynasty and changing the history
of Russia forever. Against a backdrop of the First World War and
the rumblings of a burgeoning revolution, this semi-literate
Siberian mystic had come to exercise a malign, almost hypnotic
power over the last Tsar and Tsarina of Russia, Nicholas II and
his consort, Alexandra.

Variously regarded as a saint, a sinner and a devil by those
who knew him, Grigori Yefinovitch Novykh was born in 1869
into a peasant family in the village of Pokrovskoe, deep in the
vast, little-populated wastelands of Siberia. Uneducated – he
never went to school – the young Grigori was virtually illiterate.
He was, however, rowdy and lascivious, a drinker, a brawler and
a thief, and thereby acquired the name 'Rasputin', from the
Russian word rasputnik, meaning libertine or debauched person.

Yet his life was to change forever when, after a visit to a monastery in the Urals he, 'perceived the Divine Grace' as he himself described this epiphany. There, he became fascinated with the Russian Orthodox faith, and at the same time discovered his ability to calm people in distress and to predict the future. He gave up drinking, smoking and eating meat, and began to test himself with severe fasting. His conversion to a 'Man of God' was sealed once he discovered the Khlysty, an extreme quasi-Christian sect. The Khlysts believed that only by actively sinning could one eventually reach a state of purification and be truly purged. Stress was laid on penitence, but also on ecstatic communal rites and dancing, often culminating in wild sex orgies involving the entire group.

Whether driven by religious fervour or by more basic human urges, Rasputin plotted the corruption of women from nearby villages and even had a cabin built in a remote spot to ensure the secluded seduction of hundreds of impressionable girls. Even so, his adherence to the Khlysts' hybrid of mysticism and eroticism did not entirely strip him of familial instincts. He married a local girl named Proskovia, who bore him two daughters, Maria and Varvara, and a son, Dimitri. He was not destined to play the doting father for long, however.

Rasputin now styled himself a starets or holy man. Reverence for startsy was an age-old tradition in Russia, deeply ingrained in the collective consciousness. Yet a starets was not a priest or monk but, as Dostoevsky wrote in The Brothers Karamazov, 'someone who takes your soul, your will and makes them his. When you select your starets, you surrender your will and give it to him in utter submission, in complete self-renunciation.' Rasputin was to embrace this belief wholeheartedly.

He sought to capture the minds and souls of simple-minded believers, high and low, rich and poor, in order to bend them to his will. Preaching a doctrine of salvation through sin, he emphasized to his flock, which was largely composed of women, that sins of the flesh were especially efficacious for achieving God's forgiveness, and thus salvation. Fixing them with his hypnotic eyes – and all contemporary sources agree about the extraordinary penetrating quality of his gaze – he urged them to yield unresistingly to temptation, offering himself as both the means of temptation and the vehicle for their lapse into sin.

Playing upon the general reverence for a starets and upon his mystical powers of suggestion and hypnosis, Rasputin travelled through Russia preaching and fornicating.

As the twentieth century dawned, rumours of the remarkable starets began to filter beyond the borders of Siberia. In 1903 Rasputin arrived in St Petersburg. Now in his early thirties, he presented an imposing, if shaggy, figure, clad in a sable coat thrown over peasant blouse, trousers and boots. His untrimmed and filthy hair and beard, laced with bits of food, gave off, it is said, a potent odour reminiscent of a goat. None the less, he joined the St Petersburg Theological Academy, where he came to the attention of Father Ioann of Kronstadt. The influential priest gave his blessing to Rasputin, calling him a 'God seeker'.

It was not God that he sought, however. Not long after his arrival in St Petersburg, Rasputin began to gather around him a group of noblewomen who, having heard about the strangely charismatic starets, sought his company and, through his crude lovemaking, his blessings. Largely uneducated, except in social graces, often rather empty-headed, or simply bored with their privileged, over-protected lives, many of these women found it titillating to be ravished by this malodorous peasant. Rasputin ate with his hands, tore at his food with blackened teeth and used the foulest language in their presence. He took them quickly and brutally, muttering, 'Now, Mother, everything is in order.'

The city to which Rasputin came – the capital of the Russian Empire since the days of Peter I 'the Great' – was at the beginning of its Silver Age, an era marked by shocking scandal and extreme debauchery. The artists and intellectuals of the time had embarked upon a voyage not only of intellectual and artistic discovery, but also of unrestrained sexual exploration. Suicide, murder, opium and alcohol all formed an integral part of life in the upper echelons of St Petersburg society.

Tsar Nicholas and his German-born wife, the former

Princess Alix of Hesse and by Rhine, styled in the Russian form Alexandra but known to her intimates as Alix, created for themselves a very different world. Refusing to live at the Winter Palace in the capital, where the Romanov dynasty had resided since the building's completion in 1762, Alix had created a home for them at the Alexander Palace in Tsarskoe Selo, half an hour's train ride from St Petersburg. She attempted to confine her children and Nicholas in a sort of everlasting cosy tea party, and thereby created a world for them as unhealthy as it was unreal, divorced from contact with the realities of their increasingly turbulent country. Strange and questionable characters came and went, preying upon the Tsarina's faith in charlatan healers and spurious holy men.

Initially, the Tsarina had turned to faith healers to help her bear a son. She had four daughters, the Grand Duchesses Tatiana, Olga, Militsa and Anastasia, but there was no male heir to the Romanov dynasty. In desperation she turned to a Doctor Philippe, who had three convictions in his native France for practising medicine without a licence. Philippe claimed to be able to see into the future and to communicate beyond the grave. Eventually forced to leave Russia after a series of false predictions, the royal couple were sorry to see him go, although he promised that, 'Someday you will have another friend like me who will speak to you of God.'

On 30 July 1904 Alix finally gave birth to a son, whom they named Alexei. By September, however, the royal couple were concerned by, 'the constant bleeding from his navel' and the Tsarevich was found to be suffering from haemophilia. Medical experts from all over Europe had little comfort to offer. Nicholas and Alix turned to Dr Zhimsarian Badmaev, a Tibetan herbalist, as well as to outright fakers and itinerant 'holy men' but neither modern science, Tibetan herbs nor mystics could cure the boy.

Rasputin was already nearing middle age when he came to the attention of Nicholas and Alix. He had a group of oddly assorted sponsors in St Petersburg – the Bishop Feofan (who would eventually denounce him as immoral), certain Montenegrin princesses and a highly influential intimate of the

Tsarina named Anna Vyrubova. She had been brought out of a coma by Rasputin following a riding accident, and revered him as a saint.

When the Grand Duchesses Militsa and Anastasia, who had discovered Dr Philippe years before, began to sing Rasputin's praises, backed by Anna Vryubova, the starets was summoned to the royal presence. The date was 1 November 1905, and Tsar Nicholas recorded the meeting in his diary: 'Had tea with Militsa and Stana [Tatiana]. Met a man of God, from Tobolsk province.' It was to be the start of a fateful association.

For a couple of years meetings between Rasputin and the royal family were rare. In the meantime, however, his fame in St Petersburg grew. Even the Prime Minister, Peter Stolypin, who had no time at all for mysticism and was to become one of the holy man's most bitter opponents, invited Rasputin to pray at the bedside of his sick daughter.

Rasputin cut an exotic figure in the fashionable salons of Russian society. He attracted women to him easily with an inner power that they found difficult to resist. Then there were his eyes . . . According to Maurice Paléologue, France's Ambassador to Russia at the time, 'The whole expression of his face was concentrated in the eyes – light-blue with a curious sparkle, depth, and fascination. His gaze was at once penetrating and caressing, naïve and cunning, direct and yet remote. When he was excited, it seemed as if his pupils became magnetic.'

As his fame spread, the aura of disturbing stories about his incredible erotic adventures fanned the lustful imaginations of the aristocracy. Despite the stench of scandal that surrounded him, the royal family continued to meet with Rasputin – though only in private. In a small stone house in Tsarskoe Selo belonging to the devoted Anna Vyrubova, Nicholas and Alix would come to listen, enraptured by the holy man's words. At the end of 1907, the young Tsarevich, Alexei, started bleeding, and for the first time Rasputin was summoned to his bedside. Amazingly, his presence immediately calmed the boy, and his internal bleeding slowed and eventually stopped. The Tsarevich's illness had fatally chained the Tsar's family to the notorious starets forever.

But as Rasputin drew ever closer to the royal family, educated, refined society began to grumble. After a time, the rows and scandal surrounding the Tsarina's holy man attracted the attention of the Dowager Empress, the widow of the Tsar's father, Nicholas I. As a young woman she had been told a prophecy which foresaw that: 'Your son will reign, will be climbing the mountain to attain wealth and great honour. Only he will never reach the top, stricken by a muzhik's hand.' But Nicholas and Alix had already formed their own, unshakeable opinion of Rasputin and refused to heed the Dowager's order that, 'the fiend incarnate be banished from St Petersburg.'

Rasputin's rise to power within the imperial court had begun as Russia was attempting to establish a constitutional monarchy. In the wake of the country's humiliation in the disastrous Russo-Japanese War of 1904-5, public pressure had forced the Tsar and his advisers to establish the Duma, Russia's first parliament. A year later Nicholas had appointed a new Prime Minister, Peter Stolypin. Russia prospered under his guidance, but to the Tsarina he was an arch-enemy. She hated him because he dared to vilify her beloved Rasputin. Stolypin repeatedly told the Tsar that he needed to distance himself and his family from this untrustworthy man. At one point, he even brought to the Tsar documented proof of Rasputin's evil affairs. Nicholas, however, ignored him, not wanting to take away from Alix the one man she believed could save her son's life. Thwarted, Stolypin therefore decided to take action himself. He ordered the starets to leave the capital, thus further outraging the Tsarina. Rasputin left St Petersburg, beginning a journey to Jerusalem and the Holy Land.

His banishment from the capital was to be short-lived, however. On the evening of 1 September 1911, during a royal performance of Rimski-Korsakov's Tale of the Tsar Saltan at the Kiev Opera House, Stolypin was shot at point-blank range by a revolutionary, Bogrov. Nicholas had lost the last truly able statesman to serve him.

In October 1912, while the Tsar and his family were at their hunting lodge in Spala, Alexei fell and struck the side of a bathtub. Bruised and bleeding, he was in terrible pain, and a notice announcing his death was drawn up. Desperate, the Tsarina telegraphed Rasputin. 'God has seen your tears,' he wired back. 'Do not grieve. The Little One will not die.' Hours later, Alexei's temperature fell and the bleeding stopped. To Nicholas and Alix it was a miracle sent directly from God, and Rasputin's future as a holy man in whom the Tsarina placed absolute confidence was assured.

With his position in the palace secure under the Tsarina's protection, Rasputin became increasingly powerful and untouchable. The Tsarevich's illness was a closely guarded secret, but the complete ignorance of the Russian people about Alexei's disease – and, hence, the reasons for the Tsarina's confidence in Rasputin – created a threatening situation. All sorts of fantastic tales about vast debauches at Tsarskoe Selo, in which the women of the royal family and their followers gave themselves to Rasputin in a frenzy of lust, began to circulate.

The censors did their best to hide this embarrassing upstart. They daubed ink over newspaper columns that carried stories about or referring to him. The black blotches came to be known as 'caviar', but readers knew whom the caviar were protecting, and they invented stories of their own. The talk centred on his position at the very pinnacle of society. 'The filthy gossip about the Tsar's family has now become the property of the street', wrote an agent of the Okhrana, the Tsar's brutal and corrupt Secret Police.

Crude cartoons were passed around portraying Rasputin emerging from the naked Tsarina's nipples to tower over Russia, his wild eyes staring from a black cloud of hair and beard. A caricature in the form of an icon showed him with a vodka bottle in one hand and the naked Tsar cradled like the Christ child in the other, while the flames of Hell licked at his boots and nubile women, naked apart from angels' wings and black silk stockings, flew about his head. A photograph of Rasputin with a collection of society women was reproduced by the thousand. Mikhail Rodzianko, a leading politician, declared that he was horrified to find that he recognized many of these worshippers from high society, and added that he had received a huge mass of letters from mothers whose daughters had been disgraced by the impudent profligate.

In 1914 Russia went to war with Germany and a wave of patriotic fervour broke over the country. Nicholas was cheered wherever he went, and flags, icons and portraits of the Tsar sold out. In the capital, the German Embassy was destroyed by the fervent mob.

Over the next two years the government went through four Prime Ministers and six Ministers of the Interior, many of whom had been happy to pay large sums to Rasputin for their position. As a consequence of Rasputin's and Alix's meddling in state affairs, and Nicholas's acquiescence, Russia's government was deprived of every reasonably able statesman. By the autumn of 1916, the behaviour of the Tsarina and her holy man had left Russia with a motley assortment of rogues, incompetents, nonentities and madmen at the heart of government. Rasputin arranged for the appointment of placemen to key government posts, often selected for the most trivial of reasons; Alix supported his decisions, overriding all objections, and the Tsar confirmed them. Alexei Khvostov was appointed on the basis of his fine bass voice. Rasputin's minion Boris Stürmer became Prime Minister in the autumn of 1916. Stürmer, a 'shallow and dishonest creature who emits an intolerable odour of falseness,' excited disgust. He maddened the United States Ambassador, David Francis, by gazing at himself in a mirror with enraptured admiration during appointments, twirling the waxed ends of his moustache.

The second most powerful position of state, that of Minister of the Interior, was gifted by Rasputin to Alexander Protopopov, who strutted around in high boots and an operatic uniform he had designed himself. He suffered from syphilis, was prone to hallucinations, and was considered insane.

Meanwhile, letters to the Tsar from highly placed officials overflowed with unwise or corrupt advice. Embroidered by the hand of the Tsarina, Rasputin's influence was spreading all the way to the front line, with devastating consequences. By replacing the War Minister with Vladimir Sukomlinov, a money-grabbing incompetent, but nevertheless a close friend, Rasputin signed the death warrants of thousands of Russian soldiers. A chronic shortage of weapons and supplies developed almost immediately. By early 1915, two out of three Russian soldiers were being sent to the front line without rifles, ammunition or boots. With no wire for field telephones, communication increasingly had to be by radio, but since there was also a shortage of code books, many radio messages were picked up and easily deciphered by German intelligence. As the casualties – from disease and privation as well as from enemy action – rose, people at home started to demand answers.

Russia had been heavily engaged on the Eastern Front since the outbreak of war, and her armies had suffered terrible casualties. Rasputin's refusal to sack Sukomlinov resulted in a groundswell of accusations that the German-born Tsarina and her chief adviser were colluding with the enemy.

By mid-1915 the Russian army was on the brink of collapse. As a result, Nicholas, on the advice of Rasputin and Alix, decided to assume the position of Commander-in-Chief of the Russian armies in the field. It proved a fateful decision. For the majority of Russians in those days, the Tsar was a semi-mystical, almost god-like figure – powerful, all-seeing and certainly far beyond the judgement of the masses. Nicholas ruled 130 million people who lived over more than 8.75 million square miles and the prevailing belief was that he was a divinely appointed monarch. Now his deeply flawed character, stubbornness and inability to make effective decisions became all too obvious – he lost his god-like status in the eyes of many ordinary Russians yet despite 5 million dead, and the loss of Warsaw and his Polish territories, the Tsar remained confident that the army was loyal.

Totally isolated from reality, Nicholas had stationed himself in the provincial town of Mogilev far away from the front. He had taken over a hotel and took daily walks by the river with his English setters. In the evening he watched movies. His favourite was a twenty-two reel detective serial called, The Secrets of New York. Meanwhile Rasputin's hold on the Tsarina was growing increasingly vice-like and, in the absence of the Tsar (who may have gone just to get away from the two of them), Alix became virtually the sole ruler of the Empire, along with 'the Friend'.

The troops no longer thought of themselves as Russian soldiers. They told each other that the government had been paid a billion roubles by Berlin to ensure that as few of them as possible survived the war. But their most special hatred was reserved for the German-born Tsarina; they thought she was in league with the enemy, that she talked to Germany on a radio concealed under the eaves of her palace and that she passed secrets to her sister, Princess Irene of Prussia.

The Tsarina, meanwhile, rarely left the Alexander Palace in Tsarskoe Selo. She lay for much of the time on a chaise-longue in her boudoir, a terrier at her feet. To her, Russia was the countryside and Rasputin, the honest peasant in blouse and boots, was its personification. Mail that she received from the 'real Russia' was forged by the secret police on the orders of Protopopov, Rasputin's friend. Genuine letters told a different story.

The mood on the streets of St Petersburg now became increasingly nasty. The Okhrana said that it was no longer possible to prosecute all who insulted the Tsar and Tsarina because the numbers were too great for the courts to cope. A letter sent by the London Times' representative warned that the Romanov dynasty was in danger – banners calling for their dismissal were found everywhere.

Meanwhile Rasputin, when not with Alix, was carrying on life as normal in his apartment at 64 Gorokhovaia Street, a non-descript block where he shared his stairway with a masseuse and a seamstress. The whole of Rasputin's flat bore the stamp of bourgeois well-being and prosperity yet, located near the railway station, in a modest part of town, it enabled Rasputin to preserve his image as a man of the people. Into this apartment streamed an endless number of women – all seeking favours from Rasputin. In return he received money, wine, sweets or sexual favours. He was constantly under surveillance by the Okhrana who noted down who spent the night and what bribes they bought. Worse than that the rumours about his private life, were that he was committing gross acts of public indecency. At the Iar restaurant, an infamous drinking den in Moscow, Rasputin exposed himself to a number of women and made obscene remarks. When supper was over, a drunk Rasputin talked of the Tsarina as his 'old girl' boasting that he could do anything he liked with her. Eventually he had to be dragged away by the police.

Still the royal couple refused to hear the truth about Rasputin. In September 1916 when General Dzhunovskii showed Nicholas details of his behaviour at the Iar restaurant he was sent into retirement. Purishkevich, one of the leaders of the Duma, asked all the ministers to throw themselves at the Tsar's feet and beg him to get rid of Rasputin.

On December 8 the Union of Towns, an important municipal body went into secret session. The resolution it passed read, 'the government, now become an instrument of the dark forces, is driving Russia to her ruin and is shattering the imperial throne.' Dark forces was simple code for Grigorii Rasputin. The widely distributed pamphlet was addressed to, 'Father Grigorii, new saint of the devil, reviler of Christ's teachings, ruiner of Russian land, defiler of wives and maidens.' It urged Rasputin to rejoice at the Tsar's dulled mind, the Tsarina's delectation, at their daughters' seduction and at the propagation of dark forces – 'Rejoice', the pamphlet said, 'Rejoice, foul receptacle of Satan!' Slowly they were becoming aware that nothing would break the royal couple's dependence upon Rasputin – he would have to die and very soon a new ally joined Purishkevich's cause. Prince Feliks Yusupov, a transvestite and a member of one of the most illustrious families in Russia, who carried, 'God in one eye and the devil in another'. Together they recruited Grand Duke Dmitrii Pavlovich, who had been touted as a possible husband for the Tsar's daughter, Olga, and for almost a month the three conspirators laid their plans. They used the Princess Irina Yusupova, easily one of St Petersburg's most beautiful women, as bait to lure Rasputin into a trap. Although she was not in St Petersburg at the time, Prince Felix told Rasputin that Princess Irina was coming back for a secret assignation with him. As Rasputin licked his lips at the prospect of seducing the most beautiful woman in society, Yusupov was preparing a special chamber in which to murder him.

On the ground floor of the Yusupov Palace on the River

Moika, he ordered workmen to refurbish a suite of rooms with costly Persian carpets, antique art objects and elegant furniture. There was a white bearskin rug in one corner and in the midst of this cosy arrangement Yusupov had his servants place, 'the table where Rasputin was to take his last cup of tea.'

By the night of 16 December all was ready. Cakes filled with chocolate and rose cream were lovingly prepared and laced, by a physician, with potassium cyanide. More poison was added to the glasses into which the Madeira and Marsala, Rasputin's favourite drinks, would be poured.

Sometime before midnight Yusupov set out into the snow to collect Rasputin. When Rasputin arrived he was told that the Princess Irina was still entertaining guests upstairs but would arrive shortly and, as the sounds of Yankee Doodle (played on a phonograph by the other conspirators to simulate the princess's party) drifted down from an upstairs room, Rasputin descended the staircase to await his fate.

Prince Yusupov now served Rasputin the poisoned drinks and cakes, but to his utter horror Rasputin continued to eat and drink and asked for some gypsy songs to be played. The poison was not working and some time later, having spoken with his accomplices upstairs, Yusupov fetched a revolver and shot Rasputin. He aimed at the heart and Rasputin went down on to the bearskin rug like a broken marionette. Just as the conspirators were rejoicing, however, Rasputin struggled to his feet, lurched his way up to the main floor and fell out of a side door into a courtyard. The assassins were frantic – twice they fired – and missed. By then Rasputin was almost at the gate to the street – Purishkevich, biting his left wristbone until it bled, to ensure total concentration, raised his pistol and fired twice and Rasputin fell – hit in the back and the head.

But despite the two bullets, Rasputin's life was not yet extinguished and so the conspirators tied his hands over his head and eventually dumped his body under the ice of the River Neva. An autopsy carried out shortly afterwards showed that the poison and the bullets had not killed Rasputin – the cold, icy river had claimed that privilege – his lungs were filled with water.

Within a few hours of the murder it was well known in the government and diplomatic community who the perpetrators were and they were hailed as saviours of Russia. The streets of St Petersburg resounded with exclamations of joy, and the bridge from which Rasputin's body was dumped became a popular place to take a walk.

As Alexandra vowed eternal vengeance, Nicholas was powerless to punish the perpetrators; their star was too high in the pubic firmament. Instead Yusupov was banished to his estates, Dimitrii to the Persian Front and Purishkevich, the originator of the conspiracy, escaped totally unscathed and with his prestige massively enhanced.

Faithful to the end, the Tsarina buried Rasputin at Tsarskoe Selo. The Tsar recorded in his diary, 'at 9 o'clock we drove with all the family and turned into a field where we witnessed a gloomy picture; the coffin with the body of never-to-be-forgotten Grigori, murdered by the bigots in Yusupov's house. The weather was grey with 12 degrees of frost.' However Rasputin's body would not remain to rest in peace for long; on 22 March 1917, a group of revolutionary soldiers disinterred the coffin and burned the remains.

In a letter written shortly before his death Rasputin had predicted his demise. He wrote that if common assassins killed him, then the Tsar had nothing to fear, but if he were slain by the aristocracy then none of the Tsar's family would remain alive for more than two years, but would be killed by the Russian people.

There were seventy-four days between Rasputin's death and the Tsar's abdication, and on 18 July 1918 the prediction came true when the Tsar's entire family was assassinated in a basement of an isolated farmhouse. Rasputin's death had come too late to change the course of events. In raising their hands to preserve the old regime, Rasputin's assassins, had, in reality, struck its final blow.

JOSEF STALIN

A TWENTIETH-CENTURY TYRANT

A single death is a tragedy, a million deaths is a statistic.

The mark of Stalin's evil was that he turned morality on its head: what was bad became good, what was good, bad. This was a man who lost sight of the fact that human dignity and well-being lay at the heart of all progress.

MIKHAIL GORBACHOV

In March 1953, the people of the Soviet Union were devastated by the news that the country's Head of State was dead. At the funeral of the man known as Uncle Joe Stalin, people wept openly. To the Russians, Stalin was a saviour, the great leader who had defeated Hitler's Nazis and kept the Americans at bay. As they filed past his coffin few cared to recall that Stalin had another, darker reputation, as the murderer of millions of his own people, more than the Tsars had accounted for over four centuries. A ruthless bureaucrat, Stalin turned a popular revolution, based on ideals of freedom and equality, into a totalitarian dictatorship maintained by terror.

Born Iosif Vissarionovich Dzhugashvili, on 21 December 1879, in the Caucasian town of Gori, Georgia, he was the only one of four children to survive infancy. His father, Vissarion Dzhugashvili, was an unsuccessful cobbler and drunk, who beat his son and wife. When Stalin was eleven, his father was killed in a brawl, and it was left to his mother, Katerina, to keep the family together. She took in washing and sewing, hired herself out for housework, and nursed young Joseph through smallpox, which left him facially disfigured; and septicaemia, which left his left arm slightly crippled. An illiterate peasant girl, Yekaterina was deeply religious and intent on her son training for the priesthood, one of the few careers in which the non-Russian Georgian poor might rise to higher station. He was enrolled in the local Orthodox parochial school in Gori in 1888.

Highly gifted, Stalin won a free scholarship in 1894 to the Orthodox theological seminary in Tiflis, to begin his training as a priest. But he preferred revolutionary literature to the Bible and in his fourth year joined Mesame Dasi, a secret socialist group. Expelled from the seminary in May 1899, just as he was about to graduate, Stalin first tried tutoring and then clerical work at the Tiflis Observatory.

Calling himself Koba or 'Indomitable', the young Josef joined the Social Democratic Party of Georgia in 1901 and plunged full-time into revolutionary work. He organized assassinations, strikes, demonstrations and bank robberies to swell the Bolshevik coffers. By 1902, the Okhrana, the Tsarist Secret Police had published a picture of Josef Dzugashvili – one of the most successful revolutionary operatives in southern Russia.

In June 1904 Stalin married Yekaterina Svanidze, a simple, devout peasant girl. She died of typhus on April 10 1907, leaving a son, Yakov. Yakov would later try to kill himself; a failure for which his father would mock him. Yakov would die in a Nazi concentration camp in 1943 after Stalin had refused to trade for his life. Stalin's own life between the turn of the century and 1917 was constantly in danger. He spent much of it on the run from the Tsarist authorities or in exile in the frozen wastes of Siberia. However, in March 1917, the work of Stalin and other revolutionaries in Russia and abroad paid off. Demoralized by three years of slaughter fighting the Germans in the First World War, and disaffected by years of poverty and repression at home, the Russian people rose up against the Tsar, Nicholas II. The Russian Revolution had begun.

When he heard that the Tsar had abdicated, Stalin rushed from his Siberian prison to the capital, Petrograd, known today as St Petersburg. The city was in turmoil, filled with joyous workers, mutineer soldiers and sailors and returning exiles. A provisional government under the leadership of Alexander Kerensky had taken control – to the fury of Lenin, the newly returned leader of the Bolshevik Party. The provisional government's refusal to withdraw from the war with Germany played into the hands of Lenin and the Bolsheviks. Aligning themselves with troops reluctant to go to the battlefront, Lenin encouraged an armed coup led by Trotsky, the head of the Petrograd Soviet in October 1917.

From October of that year Stalin would make himself central to the activities of the new government. It was then that he adopted the name Stalin, 'Man of Steel'. In later years, Stalin would portray himself as central to the October Revolution, but in fact he was a mere functionary. Stalin would also portray himself as Lenin's closest ally and the person directly responsible for directing the Revolution. He even had a faked photograph of himself and Lenin hanging on the wall of his dacha at Kuntsevo. During Stalin's attempts to create an important history for himself in retrospect, he first subjected the real heroes of the revolution to silence, and then had them written out of the history books. By 1937 he had disposed of thirty-seven of them in a more brutal fashion. Only those who spouted the new version of events remained.

From the moment the Soviet Union came into being it was in a continual state of crisis. Withdrawal from the War in 1918 was followed by a bitter civil war between the Revolutionary Bolshevik government and the White Army, Tsarist sympathizers supported by forces from western Europe.

During the Civil War of 1918-21 Stalin took on a huge number of mundane jobs that nobody else wanted. He was the Commissar for Nationalities, the Commissar for Rabkrin, a member of the Revolutionary Military Council, the Politburo and the Orgburo and Chairman of the Secretariat – with the result that he gained a reputation as a poor orator, a plodding theorist and a prickly character. All the Party leaders made the same mistake of underestimating Stalin's potential power, and his ambition to use it. Lenin was as guilty as the rest.

As Chairman of the Secretariat and the only Politburo member in the Orgburo, Stalin promoted his friends and dismissed opponents. During 1922 alone, more than 10,000 provincial officials were appointed, mostly on Stalin's personal recommendation. They came from humble backgrounds with little formal education.

In 1919, Stalin ran the Workers' and Peasants' Inspectorate, which gave him the power to investigate every official in the country. By 1922 there were very few Party leaders, or members of the Politburo, whom Stalin did not have under surveillance and he would use blackmail to get what he wanted. With cold, ruthless efficiency Stalin began his climb to control the Party. In April 1992 Lenin agreed to make Stalin General Secretary. It was to prove a crucial appointment for it was a position that placed Stalin perfectly for the next crisis within the new state: who would succeed Lenin as Party Leader.

Lenin first showed signs of illness in 1921, for the past four years he had been working sixteen hours a day without a break. In May 1922 he suffered a stroke and pleaded with Stalin to give him poison. But Stalin refused: Lenin was more useful to him alive.

In the next seven months Lenin became increasingly close to Stalin's greatest rival, Trotsky. When, in December, Lenin suffered another stroke, Stalin took charge. He obtained from the Central Committee an order giving him the power to keep Lenin in isolation from people and news. His secretaries were already secretly reporting to Stalin.

In the last year of his life Lenin had realized what a bad leader Stalin would be, calling him disloyal, rude, arrogant and capricious. He intended to make his feelings clear at the next Congress, but suffered another stroke that made it impossible for him to talk. However, he wrote a secret letter to be read out. Realizing how fatal this would be to his ambitions, Stalin delayed the Congress and suppressed the letter. Such are the quirks of fate; if Lenin's final stroke had not left him paralysed, Stalin's name today would only occupy footnotes in Russian history books.

The USSR's heroic revolutionary age was over, and from 1921-28 the regime plunged into the more mundane task of running the country from day to day. The Civil War of 1918-21 had had a traumatic effect on the new regime. It led to comprehensive nationalization of the economy and, politically, to the establishment of virtual one-Party rule, harsh repression of opponents of the regime, abolition of freedom of expression and association, and the growth of centralized Party bureaucracy that dominated the formal organs of government. The egalitarian, socialist aims of the Revolution were being replaced with rules more suited to the oppressive regime that was forming.

Stalin rose to power because he embodied, perhaps more than any of his old colleagues, this new spirit. Office politics, patient calculation, and compromise were all required to operate a growing bureaucratic regime. Stalin, with his restless, emotional, vain, cynical, and often vindictive temperament, and lack of physical appeal, projected everywhere in public (in imitation of Lenin) a humble air, calmness, efficiency, and fatherliness - qualities that appealed to his colleagues, to the public, and, perhaps most important of all, to his new generation of Party functionaries.

Stalin's masterstroke was that he always portrayed himself as one who implemented the will of the majority. His colleagues did not fear the power of the Party machine over which Stalin presided, but rather the attempt on anyone's part to assert the kind of personal authority Lenin had exercised. Stalin exploited this miscalculation superbly, playing carefully on the mutual rivalries and suspicions of his colleagues and helping them to oust one another, while quietly staffing local and central Party organs with his own followers.

By 1927, Stalin was in complete control of the Party and all real opposition was eradicated with Trotsky's deportation from the Soviet Union two years later. Supporters like Kamanev and Zinoviev were expelled from the Party although Stalin would wait almost ten years until he had them shot for treason and would only turn his attention to Trotsky much later. For now Stalin had a much bigger target in his sights.

He introduced his first Five Year Plan for massive and accelerated industrialization of the Soviet Union, convincing the country that they had to be strong to resist enemies, both real and imagined, who were massing to destroy their Socialist paradise. Believing that the Soviet Union was 100 years behind the West, he began to change agriculture and industry. This could only be achieved, he believed, by creating a, 'command economy' and forcing farmers and industry to modernize. All peasants were forced to join collective farms. They had to pool their machinery and livestock on large farms, which were then controlled by the State. The result was a devastating famine. Peasants burnt their crops and killed their animals, rather than hand them over. Minority groups, like the Kazakh nomads, who knew nothing of cereal cropping, were ordered to cultivate wheat on pain of execution. Nearly two million died as a result and their whole way of life was obliterated.

The State's unreasonable demands for grain, forcibly extracted, meant that the peasants starved. Those who refused to join the collectives had their houses, tools and belongings confiscated. In all, some nine million men, women and children were evicted and cast into starvation. In the south, the Ukraine was particularly badly hit by a famine effecting nearly thirty million people – some even resorted to cannibalism.

The programme was partly financed by swingeing taxes on richer peasants, the Kulaks, who had been permitted by Lenin to sell surplus food to ease shortages. Soon the Kulaks lost not only the right to sell, but also their land and livestock. Then Stalin announced the elimination of the Kulaks. Millions were ordered to join the vast state-run collectives. Millions more were herded into towns to become forced labour in the new state-owned factories. Others disappeared into the growing network of corrective labour camps. More than twenty-five million were forcibly evicted and more than three million killed. What began as an economic policy turned into a regime of terror. Between 1932-34, five million people starved to death and agricultural production fell by 15%.

The blood even seeped into Stalin's own home. On 24 March 1919, Stalin had married his second wife, Nadezhda Alliluyeva, the sixteen-year-old daughter of an old Georgian revolutionary friend, Serge Alliluyev. She bore him two children: Vasili (1919) and Svetlana (1925). At one time Nadezhda had helped Stalin, telling him secrets learned from her job as a confidential code clerk in Lenin's private office. In 1932, however, at a party in Stalin's headquarters, he insulted her in front of others. Nadezhda left the room and shot herself

A nineteenth-century engraving of Attila, King of the Huns, based on a sculpture dating from 1810, some thirteen centuries after the Scourge of God – and of Europe – had drowned in his own blood.

The Dominican friar Tomás de Torquemada, first Inquisitor-General of Spain, was the embodiment of the cruelty, injustice and terror of the Spanish Inquisition. Here, a man accused of heresy is tortured by the Inquisition. Two monks wait with quill and paper to take down the victim's confession.

Ivan IV, Tsar of All the Russias. Brutal, manipulative and wholly without compassion, he was also given to catastrophic fits of rage that helped to earn him the sobriquet 'the Terrible'.

(© BETTMANN/CORBIS)

Vlad Tepes Dracula, Prince of Wallachia. A violent warlord, he became an expert in devising new methods of torture and execution, one of which would earn him his nickname 'Vlad the Impaler'.

(© HULTON ARCHIVE)

An engraving of Francisco Pizarro, Conqueror of Peru. He destroyed the powerful Inca Empire and immeasurably enriched Spain. (© Bettmann/Corbis)

Grigori Rasputin. Scheming, malevolent, treacherous and priapic, he nevertheless exercised an almost hypnotic control over the Russian royal family. (© The Illustrated London News Picture Agency)

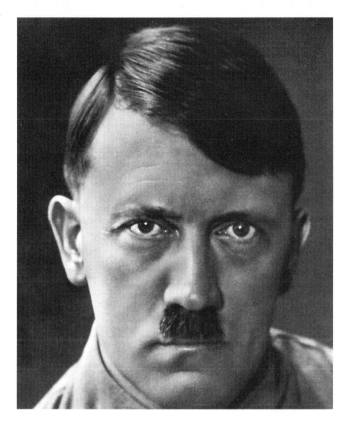

ABOVE: Adolf Hitler, leader of the National Socialist (Nazi) Party, a photograph published in 1934, the year after he became Chancellor of Germany. He brought upon the world a war of unparalleled destruction. (© THE ILLUSTRATED LONDON NEWS PICTURE AGENCY)

ABOVE LEFT: Lenin, the Soviet Union's first leader, sits with Stalin (right). The photograph is in fact a fake, combining two separate images to make Stalin appear to be Lenin's favoured son, and thereby strengthening his case when the question of succession arose after Lenin's death in 1924. (© THE ILLUSTRATED LONDON NEWS PICTURE AGENCY)

LEFT: Pol Pot, in a Khmer Rouge camp near the Thailand-Cambodia border in December 1979, after his regime, one of the most murderous in modern history, had been brought down. (© BETTMANN/CORBIS)

ABOVE: Saddam Hussein, President of Iraq from 1979 until deposed by Anglo-American forces in 2003. It is impossible to compute how many Iraqis have died as a direct result of his regime. (© PA Photos/Abaca)

ABOVE LEFT: President François Duvalier of Haiti, a country doctor who became a sinister, voodoo-practising dictator. (© Bettmann/Corbis)

BELOW LEFT: President Idi Amin Dada. To a physically imposing presence Amin added a capacity for brutality and terror made all the more sinister by the fact that, to many Western eyes, he often appeared to be little more than a figure of fun. (© Bettmann/Corbis)

Osama bin Laden, perpetrator of the atrocity that destroyed New York's World Trade Center – and more than 3,000 innocent lives – in September 2001, and now the most wanted terrorist in the world. To the enormous chagrin of the United States, he is still at large.
(© Rex/SIPA)

in the head. The official explanation was that she had died of appendicitis. Stalin did not even attend her funeral. His son, Vasilli, died an alcoholic.

Each factory or business was taken over by the State and given a target that it had to meet every year, over five years. The targets were worked out by Gosplan in Moscow. This organization consisted of half-a-million workers who did nothing but set targets for every factory and works only to then check how much was actually produced. This put immense pressure on workers and managers, but punishment for failing to meet the targets was severe. Managers of factories could be executed. Workers were forced to work longer hours and were not allowed to change their jobs. Being away from work became a crime. Many factories faked production figures, or disregarded the quality of goods produced. So long as the numbers were right, nothing else mattered. It was estimated that half of all tractors made in the 1930s broke down.

In private, Stalin was identifying himself with the great despots of history. He was fascinated by Genghis Khan, whose belief that, 'the deaths of the vanquished are necessary for the tranquillity of the victors', he concurred with. He had also taken a shine to Augustus, the first Roman Emperor, who had disguised the autocratic nature of his rule by refusing the title of King, just as Stalin was permitting himself at most the unofficial title of Leader. Those who objected to Stalin's methods ended up in the slave labour camps, the Gulags. Deliberately situated in the harshest areas of Russia, prisoners were worked to death. Huge industrial schemes like the Knieper Dam and the Bellmore Canal became a living hell for hundreds of thousands who died during their construction. By 1933 nearly a million Soviet citizens languished in forced labour camps. Further millions were in prisons, deportation camps or compulsory resettlement areas. No one was safe from being branded as an enemy and Stalin found as many enemies inside the Communist Party as he did outside.

At the seventeenth Party Congress in February 1934, 300 older Party members voted against Stalin as Party Leader and in favour of Kirov. Stalin was infuriated and his revenge was swift. In December, Kirov was assassinated – almost certainly on Stalin's orders – and then he enlarged the powers of the NKVD, the Secret Police, who began rounding up Stalin's opponents. Evidence was fabricated and the leading Bolsheviks were given 'Show Trials', where they were forced to confess to ridiculous crimes which they could not possibly have committed. Confessions were extracted under torture. Of the 1,200 delegates at that fateful Congress, over 1,100 were arrested, executed or died in the Gulag labour camps; of the one hundred and thirty nine Central Committee members, ninety eight were shot. From their headquarters in Lubyanka prison, the NKVD, under Stalin's orders, spread fear through the entire country.

The Great Terror of 1937-38, following quickly after the violent campaigns of collectivisation and industrialization, left no one in doubt about the consequences of even covert disobedience. Victims were tried by troiki, consisting of the local NKVD Chief, Party Secretary and Procurator. Trials were derisory and brief and sentences carried no right of appeal. As the terror intensified, anybody who held a political, administrative or managerial post lived in fear.

Between one, and one-and-a-half million people were killed by firing squad, physical maltreatment or massive overwork in those two years alone. Vans and lorries marked 'Meat' or 'Vegetables' would carry the victims out to a quiet wood, where shooting grounds and long, deep pits had been secretly prepared. Trains, full of victims, would pass through towns at night to avoid public scrutiny. The terror was chaotic and confusing – thousands went to their death not knowing what they had done and shouting their loyalty to Stalin – their Man of Steel.

The Soviet Union in the 30s will be remembered above all for its bloody purges of all areas of society: political and private. From 1934-38 at least 7,000,000 people disappeared. These included the Bolshevik leaders whom Stalin had forced out from 1925 to 1927, poets, scientists, managers of industries who did not meet their targets for production and millions of ordinary Soviet citizens. It would not have taken place but for

Stalin's personality and ideas. He directed the state's machinery against, 'anti-Soviet elements' and, 'enemies of the people'. In order to sustain his industrialization plans, he needed to keep his mines, timber forests and construction sites constantly supplied with slave labour.

Next Stalin turned to the army. He wanted to ensure that only his own policies were being promoted and by the time the military purge was over, nearly 40,000 officers had been arrested, almost 15,000 shot and the rest sent to the camps to die. Practically the entire High Command of the armed forces was obliterated.

Even exile abroad would provide no haven. Stalin's political bete-noir, Trotsky, was tracked down to Mexico in August 1940 where NKVD agents murdered him with an ice pick. Stalin wanted to wipe out all opponents, but more so all those long-serving Party members who knew that his glorious past was a fiction and he was not Lenin's true successor. Stalin claimed that he alone had been responsible for the successes in the Civil War.

No unit of social life – including the family – would be free from Stalin's control. Denunciation became the order of the day. Young girls were rewarded for betraying their fathers to the authorities, even when his crime was as lowly as having stolen two potatoes from a collective farm. Even harmless old peasant women muttering their dissatisfaction about housing standards would be dispatched to the Gulags. Casual jokes against Stalin or the state were treated as treason. Every citizen was a target.

By 1939 the whole fabric of Russian society was under threat and Stalin began to realize that if the Soviet State fell apart, his career would be over. However, although Stalin's terror eased up in 1939, there was to be little respite in the slaughter. Despite a treaty of non-aggression that had been signed between Stalin and Hitler in 1939, on 22 June 1941, Germany invaded Russia. The effect was devastating and Stalin was almost completely unprepared, due for the most part to his unwillingness to listen to reports that Hitler wanted to conquer Russia. Weakened by the purges in the 30s, the Red

Army had no effective leadership and its armies were annihilated by the better-armed and better-led Nazis. Long-silent church bells rang out in occupied towns as people celebrated their freedom whilst disillusioned Russian troops surrendered in droves. In less than six months, the invading army of just over three million had captured nearly four million of the Red Army. Behind the lines, rumour, confusion and panic began to spread.

But Hitler threw away his chance to capitalize on Russian misery, and refused to allow 800,000 Russian volunteers to fight for Germany. Freed towns were soon appalled at the cruelty of the invading forces. The Nazis were besieging Leningrad and were less than a mile from the Kremlin in Moscow. Stalin appealed over the radio to, 'his friends' the Russian people to help him throw off the yoke of Nazism, and with the onslaught of the icy clutches of winter, the tide began to turn. However, even as the Russian people laid down their lives for the Motherland, Stalin found ways of terrorizing them. During the Battle for Stalingrad, the most savage conflict of a merciless war, Stalin formed units of the NKVD who were ordered, on pain of death, to advance behind the Russian troops. If any soldiers tried to retreat they were to be shot. Soldiers were forbidden to surrender and their families, if they did, would lose their state allowances. Tens of thousands of deserters lost their lives in this way.

By 1945 the position had changed and the Red Army pushed west destroying Hitler's armies and arrived at the gates of Berlin in May. But Stalin's repression followed them. Alarmed that his troops would become contaminated by the ideas of the American and British troops in Germany, he arrested those who had even embraced their fellow victors, sending them to labour camps for re-education. This was Stalin's reward for the sacrifice of twenty million dead. More than three million Russians had escaped to the West by 1945, by 1948 almost all had been forcibly repatriated. When they got back to the USSR thousands were marched straight off the boats and trains into makeshift execution yards. At ports on the Crimea, Soviet air force planes flew low to try and drown out the sound of gunfire. Those who escaped the quayside massacres were bundled into a closed train for a lingering death in the Gulags.

For the rest of the world the consequences of Stalin's victory would be forty years of Cold War, as, in Churchill's words, an, 'iron curtain' descended on Europe, separating democratic western Europe from the Communist east. Russia's isolation in the grip of a dictator was complete.

The Soviet victory in the Second World War came at a terrible price. It has been estimated that deaths stood at twenty six million, over 800,000 had died in the siege of Leningrad alone while 622,000 had died in the labour camps. One in eight of the pre-war population was dead.

Ironically, the more severe Stalin became, the more he was revered by the people. A combination of propaganda and the ever-present threat of persecution turned him into a demigod and his rule depended upon the presence of enthusiastic support in society. As Stalin fully developed the cult of personality, kindergarten children learned nursery rhymes extolling their great leader. The idea was that the Russian people owed everything to the Party, to the State, and to the Leader. The people had to continually thank Stalin for all the theoretical gifts and presents, the social services, the jobs and lives. Slogans like, 'Thank You Comrade Stalin for a happy childhood' were widespread. One of the most iconic images of Stalin was, 'Friend of the Little Children'. Taken in the Kremlin in 1936, Stalin was pictured holding six-year-old Gelya Marikova. Ironically a year later, Gelya's father, Ardan, was executed on Stalin's orders, accused of spying for Japan. Soon after, Gelya's mother was shot as the wife of an enemy of the people. Authorities erected loudspeakers in public streets so that announcements could be broadcast. The Cult of Stalin served a definite political purpose. It provided a focus of loyalty and patriotic feeling. The Tsar-like image of Stalin was useful in affirming that the State had a strong, determined leader. The only art that Stalin would permit was Socialist Realism, which he said, 'aided the process of ideological transformation in the spirit of socialism' and he made sure there were plenty of vast pictures of himself all over Russia.

By 1956, 706 million copies of Stalin's works had been published. In 1949 at a parade in Red Square, to celebrate his seventieth birthday, an image of his face was projected into the sky above the Kremlin. The perfect Stalin was everywhere while the real Stalin hid himself from view.

The end of the war had marked a turning point in Stalin's psychology; he was deified by his people but became increasingly paranoid and insecure. He employed fifteen personal food tasters. His tea had to come from specially sealed packs, which were used just once. When a woman who always prepared his tea was spotted taking leaves from a pack with a broken seal, she was thrown into Lubyanka prison. Tunnels were dug to link his office with other government buildings. When forced to appear above ground, he used only an armour-plated car with bullet-proof windows three-inches thick.

As Stalin's paranoia grew, so did his wrath. The persecution of Party operatives and citizens alike continued. Even his own relatives died. In Leningrad, sensing the over-confidence of the Communist Party there, Stalin executed 2,000 Party workers. Central Soviet leadership was like a gang, and Stalin as its leader relied upon its fellow members to organize the State's institutions. Competence and obedience were pre-requisites. The penalty for disagreement was, 'seven grams of lead' in the head. Even his most trusted and long-serving ministers were not exempt. The wife of Stalin's private secretary was shot and he was dispensed with. The Head of State's wife spent seven years in a prison camp to guarantee her husband's behaviour, and Molotov's wife was sent to the Gulags. A year before her arrest in 1949, Stalin had told Molotov that he should divorce her on the grounds that she was Jewish. Stalin thought that the Jews were a, 'dangerous alien element who were loyal to Israel' rather than to him. When his daughter, Svetlana, fell in love with a Jew, Stalin had him labelled a British Agent and dispatched to an Arctic labour camp. Recent research suggests that Stalin had, in fact, like Hitler, devised his own Final Solution.

Having been brought to the brink of extinction by the Nazis, the Jews were to be Stalin's next target; in fact the years

1948-53 were to be black ones for Soviet Jewry. Jewish theatres and journals were closed and Jewish intellectuals arrested. The medical profession was another vehicle for his paranoia. In what has become known as the 'Doctors Plot', Stalin persecuted Jewish physicians, arresting them on charges of poisoning people with drugs and killing them on the operating table. Ironically, it was Stalin's persecution of the Jewish doctors and the atmosphere of fear that surrounded him, which contributed to his death.

As he lay dying from a stroke in the bedroom of his dacha outside Moscow on March 2 1953, his staff were too frightened to disobey his orders and enter his room. Early intervention could have saved his life, but he lay there for almost twelve hours until a guard entered. His personal physician, Professor Vinogradov was in chains in Lubyanka prison, being beaten on Stalin's orders. The doctors who were called were unfamiliar with his medical history. He was beyond salvation and died on 5 March.

Through a succession of bulletins, the Soviet people had been made aware that Stalin was gravely ill. At four in the morning of 6 March 1953, it was announced, 'The heart of the comrade-in-arms and continuer of genius of Lenin's cause, of the wise leader and teacher of the Communist Party and the Soviet Union, has ceased to beat.'

Stalin's body was washed by a nurse and then carried via a white car to the Kremlin mortuary. There, an autopsy was performed. After the autopsy was completed, Stalin's body was given to the embalmers to prepare it for the three days it would lay in state. Thousands of people lined up in the snow to see it. The crowds were so dense and chaotic outside that some people were trampled underfoot, others rammed against traffic lights, and some others choked to death. From under the glass, the chemically treated body could still terminate innocent lives.

The exact death toll during Stalin's years in power is estimated as tens of millions, but it is a measure of the fear he invoked and the propaganda sleight-of-hand he performed, that his funeral was the scene of the most extraordinary grief.

Stalin had taken Russia from the wooden plough to the nuclear age in thirty years. He had caught up with the advanced countries that had spent centuries making the transition. But in the process, the lives of more than twenty million Soviet citizens had been sacrificed. Another fourteen million languished in the Gulag camps at the time of his death.

ADOLF HITLER

FATHER OF THE FINAL SOLUTION

I am responsible for the fate of the German people, I am the supreme Justice...and everyone must know that for all future time that if he raises his hand to strike the state, then certain death is his lot.

ADOLF HITLER

At the end of the Second World War, Germany lay in ruins. The Führer, Adolf Hitler, lay dead in a Berlin bunker, killed by his own hand. The monstrous dictator who had manipulated the minds of the masses had promised his people a brave new world and a bright new future. Instead, he murdered their sick relatives, persecuted gypsies, homosexuals and the disabled, and instigated the Final Solution, which saw the slaughter of nearly six million Jews. To the world he brought a war of unparalleled destruction, a war that would claim the lives of more than forty million people. Over half of them were civilians.

Adolf Hitler was born at 6.30 p.m. on the evening of 20 April 1889 in the small town of Brasnau on the frontier of Austria and Bavaria. The Europe he was born into was controlled by the Hapsburg Empire – one of the four great empires that ruled over central and eastern Europe. Hitler's family, on both sides, came from the Waldviertel, a poor, remote country district, cut off from the main arteries of Austrian life.

Adolf was the third child of his father's third marriage. Alois Hitler, a customs official, was hard, unsympathetic and short-tempered and much older than Adolf's mother, Klara. Faithfully protective of his mother, Adolf found his father a boorish brute. He went to school where it was reported that, 'he lacked self-discipline, was arrogant and bad-tempered. He reacted with ill-concealed hostility to advice or reproof; at the same time, he demanded of his fellow pupils their unqualified subservience, fancying himself in the role of leader.' But he left school without a leaving certificate. It was a failure that was to rankle for a long time.

After living at home for a while, Adolf went to Vienna and stayed there from 1909-13. He applied to the Vienna Academy of Art and the Academy of Architecture, but was rejected, so instead spent his time lounging around cafes and joining in every discussion on politics and philosophy. These were among his most formative years, when his character and opinions were taking definite shape. He lived in a dosshouse near the river for most of the time, making just enough money to live on by drawing posters and crude advertisements for small shops. He was a loner with few friends or acquaintances, a fringe character convinced of his own artistic talents and embittered by the bourgeois society which had rejected him.

In 1913 Hitler left Vienna for good. He was twenty-four years old, awkward, moody and reserved, yet nursing a passion of hatred and fanaticism, which from time to time broke out in a torrent of excited words.

To avoid conscription into the Austrian imperial army, he moved to Munich and found lodgings with a tailor's family. He was still living in a fantasy world, brooding and muttering about his theories on race and then bursting out into wild rages against the priests, the Jews, and the Hapsburgs. The Jewish people, Hitler was convinced, were conspiring to destroy and subdue the Aryan people as an act of revenge for their own inferiority. Sadly, the Jews were an easy target in the first half of the twentieth century as more and more of their peasant communities in Russia and eastern Europe were being driven west by the pogroms.

In 1914, patriotic crowds gathered in German streets to celebrate the outbreak of the First World War. Amongst them was the twenty-five-year-old Hitler. Though still an Austrian citizen he succeeded in joining a Bavarian infantry regiment. War offered Hitler the chance to slough off the frustration, failure and resentment of the past few years. Throughout the war Lance-Corporal Hitler served as a Meldeganger, (a runner) whose job it was to carry messages between Company and Regimental HQ, and he was awarded two Iron Crosses for bravery. The years between 1908-18 hardened Hitler and when he emerged it was with a stock of fixed ideas and prejudices which were to alter little for the rest of his life. He had acquired an even stronger hatred of the Jews; contempt for the ideals of democracy, internationalism, equality and peace; a preference for authoritarian government and faith in the heroic virtues of war. Most important of all, he had hit upon a conception of how political power was to be secured and exercised which, when fully developed, was to open the way to a career without historical parallel. It just required a shock to precipitate it – and that came with the end of the war, the capitulation of Germany and the overthrow of the Hapsburg Empire.

The period after the end of the First World War was one of widespread unrest in Europe as the political and social structure of half a continent was thrown into the melting pot. Few towns were as sensitive as Munich – its political atmosphere was unstable and veered from one extreme to another. Such was the promising political setting for Hitler to begin his career.

Hitler got a job as an army Instruction Officer, with the brief to inoculate the men against socialist, pacifist or democratic ideas. His first task was to investigate the extremist German Workers' Party. On the evening of 12 September 1919, Hitler attended his first meeting in a Munich beer cellar where twenty-five people had gathered.

The German Workers' Party was an ideal vehicle for Hitler – it was a Party at the bottom of the pile and so he had a chance to play a leading part. He offered his services and slowly pushed the Party forward until, in 1920, he resigned from the army to devote himself to building up the Party. He had an unusual talent for articulating the most vulgar populist prejudices and the self-awareness and self-confidence of the political agitator began to take shape. He learned to lie with conviction, to dissemble with candour and his distrust was matched by his contempt. Men were moved by fear, greed, lust for power, envy, often by mean and petty motives; politics,

Hitler concluded, was the art of knowing how to use these weaknesses for one's own ends.

Hitler's bloodthirsty speeches struck a chord. Party attendance first doubled and then trebled. In a short time, Hitler was able to bully his way into becoming the undisputed leader of the Party, which was renamed the National Socialist German Workers' Party (NSDAP – Nationalsozialistisch Deutsche Arbeiterpartei), or Nazis for short. In the beer halls of Munich, Hitler recruited an army of thugs called the Sturmabteilung (the Brownshirts), or SA. Their purpose was to spread terror, intimidation and violence on to the city streets. In meetings they would act as Hitler's bodyguard, mercilessly beating up anyone who questioned his words. While his brutish gangs ruled the streets, he began a campaign to charm respectable society.

Hitler could play the game at a lot of different levels, he had a kind of folksy earnestness that appealed to the lower classes and he moved very easily in society drawing rooms. Ladies clearly found him attractive and were amongst his most important benefactors, giving him money and jewellery to further his political cause.

Hitler also encouraged his female supporters by presenting himself as a hermit-like, celibate figure who devoted all his energies to the good of Germany. But again, the image he projected was a lie for, at the time, he was involved with a number of teenage mistresses, beginning with Maria Reiter, the daughter of an innkeeper from Bertesgaden. He was thirty-seven and she was sixteen, so she was literally young enough to be his daughter. The mistress who made the biggest impression on Hitler, however, was sixteen-year-old Geli Raubal. Geli was Adolf's niece, the daughter of his half-sister, Angela. In 1929, Geli moved into her Uncle Adolf's grand apartment on Munich's Prinzregentemplatz. She took a bedroom adjoining his on the second floor. Geli was a vivacious, idealistic free spirit in contrast to Hitler's controlling, strict and possessive personality. Geli soon felt trapped, but Hitler would not let her go. The longer they were involved the more she saw of his nasty side. On 19 September

1931, Geli was found dead in Hitler's apartment. She was bleeding from a wound near her heart. One arm was stretched out towards a pistol, a wolfer 6.35. The police recorded a verdict of suicide.

Geli was the first of Hitler's mistresses to be driven to a violent death, but she would not be the last. The actress Rennate Muller threw herself to her death from a window in 1937, and Eva Braun attempted suicide at least once before her final pact with Hitler. However it was Geli's picture that Hitler kept in his bedroom in Munich and in Berlin until his death in 1945.

Four years after the end of the First World War, Germany was still a troubled, distracted and divided nation. But events were on the side of the extremists. Germany was crippled by the massive reparations owed under the Treaty of Versailles made at the end of the First World War and the nation's inability to pay meant the rapid acceleration of inflation. At the end of 1918 the German mark had stood at four to the dollar, by 1923 there were 7,000 marks to the dollar.

Nazism was a phenomenon that thrived in conditions of disorder and, in 1923, two new factors made their appearance, which brought Germany to the verge of economic and political collapse. The first was the occupation of the Ruhr by France and the second was the total collapse of the mark. The French occupation united the German people as they had never been united before, and by 1 November the mark stood at 130 thousand million to one dollar. This meant food shortages, bankruptcies and unemployment. Economic collapse reached down and touched every member of society in a way which few political events ever can.

In 1923 the Nazi Party began holding a series of rallies in Bavaria; however, Hitler was sentenced to five years in prison for attempting to overthrow the Bavarian government. The Party was dissolved, but not for long. At the end of 1924 Hitler was released from custody and reformed the Party.

He now set himself two objectives: to establish absolute control over the Party and to make it a serious force in German politics. The process was to prove a slow one. Germany was making an astonishing economic recovery, but fortunately for

Hitler, disaster was just round the corner. In 1932 the global depression hit Germany hard. Unemployment soared to well over six million and countless Germans saw the apparently solid framework of their existence cracking. In such circumstances men entertain fantastic fears and extravagant hopes, and it was under these conditions that the fantastic demagogy of Hitler began to attract a mass following. When it came to the elections, the Germans needed a radical solution. The solution they chose was Hitler and the Nazi Party. Hitler portrayed himself as a Messiah whose role it was to lead the German people to a type of paradise on earth.

On the morning of 20 January 1933, Adolf Hitler, the petty-official's son from Austria, the down-and-out of the Home for Men, became Chancellor of the German Reich. Nazi propaganda later built up a legend which represented Hitler's coming to power as an upsurge of great national revival. The truth is more prosaic. Despite the mass support he won, Hitler came to power as a result of a shoddy political deal. He did not seize power; he manipulated his way into office by Machiavellian intrigue. Within a few weeks, Hitler had banned the Communist and Social Democratic Parties, dissolved the Catholic Centre and right-wing Nationalists and taken over the trade unions, five of the most powerful organizations in Germany. His gangster methods, with the crude and uninhibited use of force in the first, not in the last, resort, had produced astonishing results. Any opposition in the cabinet dissolved before the wave of violence, and by the summer of 1933 Hitler was complete master of the German Government.

In 1934 Hitler started a chain of events that led to a purge within the army and SA in Germany. How many were killed will never be known as all documents were burnt, but the figure is believed to be around five hundred. When he was asked why the men had not been tried before execution, he replied that, 'I am responsible for the fate of the German people, I am the supreme Justice…and everyone must know that for all future time that if he raises his hand to strike the State, then certain death is his lot.' Hitler had with one blow removed the pressure on him from both the Left and the Right, and could proceed to deal with the problem of the Succession. By the time that President Von Hindenburg died on 2 August, all had been arranged. Within an hour came the announcement that the office of President would be merged with that of Chancellor and that Hitler would become the Head of State as well as Supreme Commander in Chief of the Armed Forces of the Reich. On the same day the officers and men of the German Army took the oath of allegiance to their new Commander in Chief. The form of the oath was significant because they were called on to swear allegiance not to the Constitution, or to the Fatherland, but to Hitler personally.

On 19 August 1934, Germany went to the polls and the Führer, as Hitler was now to be known, swept in with a majority of nearly 90 per cent of the votes – out of forty-six million voters, only around four million had had the courage to vote against him. The Nazi revolution was complete; Hitler had become the dictator of Germany.

But Hitler's new German paradise was not a place where everyone was welcome. From the very beginning Hitler's propaganda had portrayed the Jewish people as everything that was wrong in German society. In one film the Jews are compared to rats: treacherous, cowardly and cruel and appearing in large swarms. In 1935, at a rally at Nuremberg the Law for the Protection of German Blood and German Honour was passed. This prohibited marriages or sexual intercourse between Jews and Aryans, and banned Jews from holding public office. Furthermore, in November 1938, Hitler whipped up anti-Semitic feeling into a nationwide frenzy of violence. Jewish shop windows were broken, and over a hundred Jews were killed, with over 27,000 being interned in camps, for their so-called protection. It was called the Reichskristallnacht (the empire's night of crystal). Then he re-introduced a medieval law, forcing Jews to wear a yellow star for identification.

Hitler spread his message of hate through technical devices like the radio and the loudspeaker; eight million people were deprived of independent thought and it was now possible for him to subject them to his will. No regime in history has ever paid such careful attention to psychological factors in politics.

Hitler was a master of mass emotion. At the big rallies nothing was left to chance. He used every trick and device to heighten the emotional intensity. The sense of power, force and unity was irresistible, and all converged with a mounting crescendo of excitement to the supreme moment when the Führer made his entry. Hitler had grasped what could be done with a combination of propaganda and terrorism and, in using the formidable power placed in his hands, he also had one supreme advantage over his rivals, for Hitler had neither scruples nor inhibitions. He was a man without roots, a man who admitted no loyalties, was bound by no traditions, and felt respect for neither man nor God. Hitler showed himself prepared to seize any advantage that was to be gained by lying, cunning and unscrupulousness. Wary and secretive, he distrusted everyone and believed that, '...it is not by the principles of humanity that man lives or is able to preserve himself above the animal world, but solely by means of the most brutal struggle.' Everything was the result of cold calculation.

Hitler also preserved his position in the Party by allowing rivalries to develop amongst the other leaders and applied the principle of 'divide and rule'. There was always more than one office operating in any one section and he played one department off against another. Hatred intoxicated him. Many of his speeches are long diatribes of vitriol directed against the Jews, the Marxists, the Czechs, the Poles and the French. No less striking was his constant need for praise. His vanity was unappeasable, and the most fulsome flattery was received as no more than his due. He came to believe that he was a man with a mission, marked out by Providence, and therefore exempt from the ordinary canons of human conduct. Against all the odds, and appealing to man's baser nature, Hitler succeeded in releasing the pent-up energies in the German nation, and in re-creating a belief in their future. Hitler had recognized the immense attraction to the masses of force in combination with success. However, he hated the routine work of government and so long as his suspicions were not stirred, he left the business of running the country very much in the hands of his lieutenants, though no one needed reminding where the final authority lay.

Now in complete control of the German political system, its army and its youth, Hitler was ready to take increasingly extreme steps towards his vision of a new Aryan Germany. Hitler was a hypochondriac and he had never been good at sports, yet he believed that the sick and the weak were an unnecessary burden on the rest of society. He ordered the sterilization of 400,000 gypsies, and of the disabled and the long-term unemployed; people he considered genetically substandard. At first the systematic killings were carried out by lethal injection, but, as Hitler's list of candidates for annihilation grew, a new technique for mass-murder was developed. It was tested in six provincial hospitals, where the patients were taken into the basement and told to undress. Then they were directed to the shower room. But the drain in the floor was a fake, and the pipes didn't contain water but carbon-monoxide gas. Hitler's hospitals of death claimed the lives of over 300,000 people. The bodies were never released to the relatives in case they uncovered the truth.

Having never been interested in administration, only in power, Hitler now began using the State as an instrument with which he meant to conquer Europe. From 1935 Germany began to re-arm at an alarming rate. Hitler was well aware of the rest of Europe's extreme reluctance to engage in another war and he used this to further his own position.

On 11 March 1938 German troops entered Austria, Hitler's homeland, and two days later the country became part of the German Reich. One year later Hitler invaded Czechoslovakia and the government was placed under German protection. By 1940, Hitler's armies had swept into Poland, the Netherlands, Belgium and France and in 1941 they declared war on the United States. With Europe at his feet and all need for restraint removed, Hitler now abandoned himself entirely to megalomania and the purification of Germany using his specially chosen elite, the SS.

Hitler's vision of the SS Empire was put in hand at the beginning of the war when the SS divisions numbered only three, but by the end of the war this number had risen to thirty-five, with over half a million men. They were designed as an alternative to the army and as Hitler's personal killers. Certain characteristics were established, namely the concentration camps and the einsatzkommandos, (extermination squads). By 1944, the extermination of the Jews, the first item on Hitler's programme, was well on the way to being accomplished.

At the outbreak of the war, Hitler had interned all German Jews in camps. In occupied territories, such as Poland, they were corralled in inner-city ghettos. Here they were to be worked to death, manufacturing material to help the German war effort. With constant hunger, cold and dirt it was very difficult to keep some semblance of human dignity.

But Hitler had other plans for Poland and European Russia; he wanted to populate them with German settlers. First, however, he had to get rid of the native population. Some were used to provide slave labour for the new German Empire and remained in a state of total inferiority, without rights and without education, treated literally as a sub-human race. The surplus, including all those people of education, property and position, were to be exterminated to make room for the new colonists, or left to die of starvation.

Before the war the concentration camps had been used for the 'preventative detention' of opponents of the German regime. During the war great numbers of Jews and members of the resistance movements were transported to them. Then, in 1942, Himmler, with Hitler's agreement, began to use the camps as a source of labour for armaments work, and the SS established its own factories. Certain categories of prisoners were assigned to be 'worked to death'.

Concentration camp prisoners were also used as the raw material for medical experiments by SS doctors. All were conducted without anaesthetic or the slightest attention to the victims' sufferings. They were subjected to intense air pressure, or intense cold, until the patients' lungs burst or froze to death, and a large number of investigations into racial hygiene were conducted.

More terrible than the concentration camps were the extermination camps. At Auschwitz in Poland there were four large gas chambers each accommodating 2,000 people at any one time. Here the SS used Cyclone B, crystallized prussic acid, dropped into the death chambers. It took between three and fifteen minutes for the victims to die and the Nazi butchers knew just when to move in – when the screaming stopped. But by 1944 even the vast capacity of Auschwitz for killing was not enough. In forty-six days alone during the summer of that year, between 250,000 and 300,000 Hungarian Jews were put to death at the camp, and the SS resorted to mass shootings to relieve the pressure on the gas chambers. For Hitler this was the logical realization of the views which he had held since his youth, the necessary preliminary to the plans he had formed for the resettlement of Europe on more solid racial grounds. Himmler may have organized the extermination of the Jews, but the man in whose mind so grotesque a plan had been conceived was Hitler.

Hitler was now in his fifties. His physical appearance was still unimpressive, his bearing still awkward. The falling lock of hair and the smudge of his moustache gave his face nothing of the racial superiority he was always invoking; only his hypnotic eyes betrayed the man himself. He also suffered from constant physical pain; his spine was irreparably curved and he was racked by severe spasms often lasting days. As Hitler's megalomania grew, he began to see himself as something more than human. He believed he was an agent of divine will like the Emperors of Ancient Rome. When he ordered the building of a gigantic Nazi meeting hall, it was based on Rome's Coliseum, but Hitler's building was to be twice as high and seat over 50,000 people.

By the end of 1942 Hitler's armies were fighting on many different fronts and the bombing of German industry and the losses of manpower and equipment began to exert a greater strain on the economy. Russia, like Poland and other occupied countries, was turned into a vast labour camp to provide the human material needed for German industry and agriculture. By the end of 1943, 4,795,000 foreign workers had been recruited for work in Germany, of whom 1,900,000 were Russians, 851,000 Poles, 764,000 French, 274,000 Dutch, 230,000

Yugoslavs and 227,000 Italians. Out of nearly five million workers who arrived in Germany, only 150,000 came voluntarily. Regular manhunts were organized; men and women seized from their homes, flung into cattle trucks and transported hundreds of miles. On the way thousands died of privation.

The most fortunate were those who went to farms. Those who were sent to the heavily-bombed industrial centres were housed in terrible conditions, beaten, and exposed to epidemic after epidemic. But the figure of five million did not satisfy Hitler – he demanded more and ordered increasingly ruthless measures to secure the necessary manpower.

Just under four million Russian prisoners had been taken in the opening campaign of the 1941 war and great numbers of them were deliberately left to die from hunger or cold in the cruel winter. Hitler's need for manpower reversed the policy and by the end of 1943 nearly one million Russians were working in Germany. But it could not bring the dead to life again: of more than five million Russian soldiers captured by the Germans during the war, two million are known to have died in captivity and another million are unaccounted for.

In 1943 the 270,000 men of Hitler's Sixth Army were trapped by the Red Army at Stalingrad. Hitler refused to let them retreat and, as they stared annihilation in the face, he ordered them to die like heroes. When the 90,000 survivors surrendered Hitler went berserk.

As the façade of power crumbled, Hitler reverted to his old ways. He became increasingly vulgar and his rages grew more frequent, in fact he appeared to lose all control of himself. When he screamed out abuse his face became mottled and swollen with fury and he would wave his arms around wildly and bang the wall with his fists. Then, as suddenly as he had erupted, Hitler would stop, smooth down his hair, straighten his collar, and resume conversation in his normal voice. But when he wanted to win someone over he was still capable of an eerie charm. He was a consummate actor; able to absorb himself in a role and convince himself of the truth at the time he was speaking.

Hitler was determined that Germany would never surrender. On 19 March 1944 he issued categorical and detailed orders for the destruction of all communications, rolling stock, lorries, bridges, dams, factories, and supplies. 'If the war is to be lost, the nation will also perish. This fate is inevitable. There is no need to consider the basis even of a most primitive existence any longer. On the contrary, it is better to destroy even that, and to destroy it ourselves. The nation has proved itself weak, and the future belongs solely to the winners. Besides, those who remain after the battle are of little value, for the good have fallen.' It was to be almost his final act of betrayal which fortunately was never implemented.

As day succeeded day in Hitler's isolated world of the Reich Chancellery and its garden shelter, the news grew steadily worse. Between 12 January 1945, the day on which the Russians opened their offensive in Poland, and 12 April, when the US Ninth Army crossed the Elbe, the Allies inflicted a total defeat upon the German army. By 16 April the way to Berlin was open. Hitler had lost all control over events, and by that time he could not even find out what was happening. His one answer to every proposal was; No Withdrawal. Without bothering to investigate the facts he ordered the dismissal, degradation and even execution of officers who, after fighting against overwhelming forces, were forced to give ground – even the SS were not immune. The setting in which Hitler played out his final scene was well suited to the end of so strange a history.

The physical atmosphere of the bunker was oppressive, but this was nothing compared to the pressure of the psychological atmosphere. The incessant air raids, the knowledge that Russians were in the city, nervous exhaustion and fear produced a tension bordering on hysteria, and Hitler's violent mood changes affected the lives of all those in the shelter. On the night of 26 April the Russians began to shell the Chancellery, and the bunker shook as the massive masonry split and crashed into the garden.

Facing death and the destruction of the regime he had created, the man who had exacted the sacrifice of millions of lives rather than admit defeat was still recognizably the old Hitler. From first to last there were no words of regret, or suggestion of remorse. The fault was that of others, above all that of the Jews, for even now the old hatred was unappeased. Twenty odd years had passed and taught him nothing. Hitler sat down and wrote his final testament.

Characteristically, Hitler's last message to the German people contained at least one striking lie. His death was anything but a hero's end – by committing suicide he deliberately abandoned his responsibilities and took the coward's way out. Hitler shot himself in the mouth and on his right-hand side lay his new wife, Eva Braun, who had swallowed poison. The time was 3.30 p.m on the afternoon of Monday 30 April 1945, ten days after Hitler's fifty-sixth birthday.

The Third Reich outlasted its founder by one week.

FRANÇOIS 'PAPA DOC' DUVALIER

THE QUIET COUNTRY DOCTOR

*'The Tontons Macoute,' the purser broke in with wicked glee.
'The President's bogey-men. They wear dark glasses and they
call on their victims after dark.'*

GRAHAM GREENE, *THE COMEDIANS*
(1966)

In the Caribbean sits a tiny tropical island dotted with palm trees, exotic flowers, succulent fruits. There are green mountain regions which stretch down to sandy white beaches and fertile pasturelands. Indeed, this tiny island looks much like any other tropical paradise that you might find while gliding through the azure waters of the Caribbean. But there is one significant difference. Look closely and you will discover no high-rise hotels, no pleasure beaches and no restaurants tempting you with exotic local dishes, for this is Haiti, a land that over the centuries has been torn apart by civil unrest; a land that during the late 1950s and into the 1960s suffered under one of the most vile dictatorships in world history, that of François 'Papa Doc' Duvalier.

Haiti was first discovered, leastways by westerners, by Christopher Columbus in 1492. We named it *La Isla Espanola* which was later shortened to *Hispanola*. At the time the island was populated by Arawak Indians, who referred to the place as 'Hayti' (which in translation means 'mountainous land'). Sadly, as was often the way in cases of colonization, the natives were soon being abused by the newcomers who, realizing that the island was rich in natural resources, put the Arawaks to work in the sugar cane and cocoa fields.

But the Spanish couldn't keep Haiti all to themselves for long and Britain, along with France, soon began demanding parts of the island for themselves. Finally, in the middle of the seventeenth century, after much warring, the island became a French colony. As well as being a rich source of sugar and cocoa, the island also yielded huge amounts of coffee and cotton, but the more Haiti produced, the more was wanted. In the end, desperate to keep up with demand, the French looked to Africa to supply them with labour. Suddenly, the island was swamped with slaves which, although alleviating one problem, soon caused several others. First, the slaves brought their own religion in the form of Voodoo. Voodoo was (and still is) a very powerful force for all those who adhere to its rites. Amongst other things, these involve animal sacrifice, casting spells, the walking dead and the use of dolls and pins to exact revenge. Secondly, the French treated their African slaves with huge contempt and brutality (it is reputed that over 500,000 were either flogged, starved or buried alive), which in turn caused enormous resentment within an already volatile community. Thirdly, but by no means last, the introduction of the Africans caused a third class of people to arise, the 'mulattos' (light-skinned black people) who were the result of relations between slave owners and their slaves. In later years these mulattos would form a new strata in an already complicated class system on the island, looking down upon their darker-skinned compatriots and treating them with contempt.

By 1791, the slave community had had enough of their lords and masters and a successful revolt was initiated which saw the French overthrown. So successful was the uprising that in 1804 Haiti became the first black independent nation. But the bloodshed and internecine warfare did not stop there. A man by the name of General Dessalines declared himself emperor, but when it came to abusing the people he was little better than the imperialist French and as a result he was assassinated. Next came Henri Christophe, an illiterate ex-slave, who took over the north of Haiti while a mulatto, Alexandre Pétion, ruled in the south. When Christophe died (he committed suicide by shooting himself with a silver bullet) the north and the south united and for a brief time things looked peaceful. But by 1844 the island was once again ripped apart, only this time two new countries emerged with Haiti at one end of the island and the Dominican Republic at the other. Suddenly, Haiti was thrown into a state of anarchy and between 1843-1915 it suffered under twenty-two heads of state, most of whom met with violent ends. President Guillaume Sam was the last of their number and when he was dismembered, the Americans decided it was time to invade Haiti and bring some kind of stability to the region. In fact, the US remained in the country for over fourteen years and with all their resources managed to re-build much of Haiti's infrastructure. New roads were constructed as well as schools, hospitals, sewerage systems, but the Haitians didn't look kindly upon those people they regarded as interlopers. Finally, in 1934 the Americans (at the instigation of US President Franklin D. Roosevelt) withdrew, but politically Haiti was still in a state of constant flux. It wasn't until 1957, when François Duvalier appeared on the scene and seized power that any kind of stability looked possible. But if the Haitians thought they had found a saviour in their new leader, they couldn't have been more mistaken.

Born a short distance from the National Palace during the military dictatorship of one Nord Alexis on 14 April 1907 in Port-au-Prince, François Duvalier was the son of Duval Duvalier, who worked over a period of years as a primary schoolteacher, a journalist and a justice of the peace. His mother was Uritia Abraham, a bakery employee.

During François's early years, Haiti was in a state of almost perpetual turmoil.

'When he was one year old General Antoine Simon overthrew Alexis. He was four when a revolution ousted Simon and five when an explosion reduced the old wooden Palais National, and President Cincinnatus Leconte along with it, to splinters. Duvalier was six when President Tancrède Auguste was poisoned; his funeral was interrupted when two generals began fighting over his succession. Michel Oreste got the job, but he was overthrown the following year by a man named Zamor, who in turn fell a year later to Davilmar.'[1]

The young François's childhood was unremarkable save for the fact that in a country where nine per cent of the population weren't educated, he at least received a good schooling. As a boy, he is known first to have attended the Lycée Pétion and after leaving school to have received a short apprenticeship on a newspaper called *Action Nationale* where he used the pen name Abcerrahman, which is a phonetic spelling of Abd-al-Rahman – the first caliph who established a medical school in Cordova. Later, Duvalier attended the faculty of medicine at the University of Haiti and worked for part of his doctor's internship at the Hospice Saint François-de-Sales. It was as a physician that Duvalier came by his favoured nickname of 'Papa Doc'.

On 27 December 1939, Duvalier married Simone Ovide Faine, a nurse's aide whom he had met while the two worked together in the Hospice. Simone came from very humble beginnings; born the illegitimate daughter of a mulatto merchant called Jules Faine and one of the maids in his household, she spent much of her early life in an orphanage in the hills above Port-au-Prince. Ordinarily, a young doctor would not marry beneath his class, but Simone grew into a very beautiful young woman (with a very pale skin) and the couple were united in the St Pierre Church of Pétionville just after Christmas 1939. 'It wasn't an idyllic marriage,' said Bernard Diederich, joint author of a biography of Duvalier, but nonetheless the couple produced four children: Marie Denise, Simone, Nicole and last but not least Jean-Claude (who would later become better known as 'Baby Doc' Duvalier).

From 1934 to 1946 Papa Doc worked in a series of different hospitals and clinics researching, with the aid of a US-sponsored campaign, various tropical diseases including yaws, which is a highly infectious bacterial complaint mostly found in the tropics, featuring bumps on the skin of the face, hands, feet etc. As a result of all his hard work in this area, Papa Doc began to gain a reputation as a humanitarian, someone who cared about the parlous state of the poorer elements of Haitian society. And this reputation stood him in very good stead when, between 1946 and 1950, he took over as director general of the National Public Health Service as well as Secretary of Labour. Around this time he is also believed to have become a member of *Le Groupe des Griots*, a party of writers and activists committed to Black Nationalism and Voodoo. No one could fault Papa Doc and with all his good work amongst the sick and the needy, his very name seemed synonymous with everything that was charitable in the world. He was a father figure, a benign patriarch; a doctor who would make his country 'better'.

On 22 September 1957, this innocuous-looking, soft-spoken black man, Papa Doc Duvalier (with the military's backing), was elected President of the country. In fact, four candidates had entered the race to be elected: François Duvalier, Louis Déjoie, Clément Jumelle and Daniel Fignolé. But before the voting had begun, Fignolé was sent into exile in the US, having been accused of trying to 'buy' the army. Jumelle withdrew from the race due to his (correct) belief that the military were arranging for Duvalier to win. In fact, Duvalier's victory was so overwhelming (Duvalier: 18,841 votes; Déjoie: 463) that many charges of corruption followed, though unsurprisingly none were proved.

Initially, Duvalier promised to establish a 'noirist' regime i.e. the type of rule that would bring to an end the political stranglehold that the Haitian upper classes (those who were predominately pale-skinned, wealthy, French-speaking and Catholic) had over the country. In their place he would establish a Voodoo culture more suited to the masses. Papa Doc himself was a follower and practitioner of Voodoo (indeed he was rumoured to be a *houngan* – a Voodoo sorcerer who can mediate between humans and spirits through trance-like states) as was his wife Simone, but instead of restoring order and bringing prosperity to Haiti, the country was plunged into fourteen dark, terrible years.

Worried that the military might threaten the security of his presidency, Papa Doc sacked the head of the armed forces, replacing him with an officer who was more sympathetic to his policies. Following on from this he also, after an unsuccessful attempt to overthrow him in June 1958, reduced the overall size of the army and closed down the military academy.

Then he formed a 'Palace Guard', a group of men that were

to be his own private army, but perhaps most sinister of all, Duvalier further snubbed tradition by forming, along with his chief aide, Clément Barbot, a rural militia (estimated to number in the region of 9,000-15,000 men. Formally called the Volunteers for National Security (*Volontaires de la Sécurité Nationale* or VSN) they were commonly referred to as the Tontons Macoute (derived from the Creole term for a mythological bogeyman who grabs people in the middle of the night and makes them disappear forever). According to various studies, barely two years after Papa Doc came to power, the Tontons Macoute were twice the strength of the army and were feared throughout the country not only for their murderous ways, but also for the fact that many of their number were practitioners of Voodoo. They, therefore, had the 'dark forces' working in their favour. The Tontons Macoute were mainly recruited from the capital city's vast slum areas and were only equipped with antiquated firearms. However, the fact that they didn't receive a state salary meant that they had to rely on extortion, bribery and corruption in order to make a living. This in turn led them to commit countless acts of violence. Nor did the extortion stop at the Tontons Macoute; it was prevalent in every echelon of the new government, right up to Papa Doc himself.

For far from being the timid, passive country doctor as he had at first portrayed himself, on being elected Papa Doc showed his true colours, establishing huge government rake-offs from Haiti's main industrial interests as well as using bribery as a means of fleecing hundreds of domestic businesses. Worst still, eager to control any opposition to his power base, he saw to it that his 'enemies' were sent to the notorious Fort Dimanche where, in most instances they were tortured to death. Fort Dimanche, or Fort Mort as it was nicknamed, was built during the US occupation of Haiti. It was used as a shooting range for training the military, but when Duvalier came to power the building was turned into a headquarters for training the Tontons Macoute and then became a centre for the detention, torture and/or execution of anyone whom Duvalier deemed a threat. Newspaper editors from publications such as the *Miroir* and *L'Indépendent*, as well as radio station owners and journalists were jailed on specious charges of sedition and Duvalier's henchman, Barbot, set about bombing their offices. In this way, all forms of opposition were either extinguished or driven underground for politicians and media men alike were too frightened to express their views openly.

But if François 'Papa Doc' Duvalier was a terrifying figure to the educated upper and middle classes in Haiti, he was nothing short of a demon to the uneducated peasantry. Having studied Voodoo and aligned himself behind this religion, Papa Doc milked it to the last by posing as Baron Samedi, a particularly evil Voodoo deity who could put the living in touch with the dead. Uncannily, Duvalier did look remarkably like Samedi, especially when he dressed up in similar attire to the Voodoo god who is most often depicted wearing a black top hat, black coat tails and sunglasses. Taking this one stage further, Duvalier also had posters printed that unashamedly suggested he was at one with the Voodoo spirits, Jesus Christ and God himself. Most famously, there is an image of Duvalier standing alongside Jesus Christ, who has his right hand resting on Duvalier's shoulder, with a caption underneath reading, 'I HAVE CHOSEN HIM'. That these images, alongside Duvalier's constant bombardment of the radio stations with his ranting and raving, served to cow the illiterate under-classes, is undeniable. 'François Duvalier,' writes David Hawkes in an essay written in 1997, 'was able to secure his political power by exploiting the credulity and superstition of the Haitian peasantry. He represents a phenomenon of pre-enlightenment societies: the tyrant who does not base his legitimacy on reason or democracy, but on mystical and supernatural foundations. Visiting Haiti is probably the closest one can come to visiting medieval Europe.'[2]

That Papa Doc, therefore, was a highly manipulative individual who knew just how to keep his subjects at bay, goes without saying. But he treated his friends in much the same manner; for no one ever knew quite where they stood with this man, as was proved two years after he came to power.

On 24 May 1959 Duvalier suffered a massive heart attack and fell into a coma. The best doctors were flown in from the

US to look after the president, but while he was incapacitated, Clément Barbot, the man who had helped Duvalier set up the Tontons Macoute and who now headed that organization, took over as interim leader. Barbot stepped in to his master's shoes very easily and seemed to enjoy presiding over cabinet meetings and making political decisions. But it was a bad move by Barbot. When Duvalier had fully recuperated, the dictator didn't forget quite how effectively his number one hatchet man had managed to replace him. On 14 July 1960, Barbot was arrested by his own Tontons Macoute and later taken to Fort Dimanche on charges of corruption. Imprisoned and tortured for a period of eighteen months, Duvalier then ordered Barbot be released. Now it was Barbot's turn to feel hatred towards his former ally and on 26 April 1963, in an attempt to kidnap Duvalier's children and force the president to resign, he had the children's chauffeur and two bodyguards ambushed and killed. Naturally, Duvalier was overcome by rage and immediately ordered reprisals. A bloodbath ensued.

Tontons Macoutes patrolled the streets, sirens wailing. Road blocks were everywhere. It took hours to cross town or travel up the hill to Pétionville, where the road checks were both tedious and rough. Some former army officers, having no idea of the danger they were in, drove to pick up their children at school and on their return home were arrested at road blocks and never seen again.'[3]

But Barbot evaded capture and for several weeks those loyal to Duvalier and those to Barbot played a deadly game of cat and mouse throughout Haiti. Every night after dark the Tontons Macoute would be on the prowl for their next victim until, on 14 July, Barbot regrouped and decided on a second assassination attempt. He was cornered in a sugar-cane field by the Duvalierists who then set the field alight and shot the insurgents down as they ran to escape the flames.

Unsurprisingly Barbot's attempt to remove Duvalier wasn't the only challenge to his leadership for previously, in what must surely be one of the most bizarre attempts to overthrow any government, three Haitian men, together with two Florida deputy sheriffs and three adventurers, landed on Haitian soil with the sole intention of assassinating Papa Doc. Their mission was doomed to failure from the start and all eight men were shot during the attempt. But the carnage didn't stop there, for in turn this attempted coup had devastating consequences for another of Duvalier's opponents, his former rival for the Presidency, Clément Jumelle. Believing (or concocting the belief) that Clément Jumelle's two brothers were somehow involved in this latest plot, Duvalier sent Barbot and his Tontons Macoute to kill Ducasse and Charles Jumelle. They were hunted down to a small house in Bois Verna where they were both shot to death. Afterwards photographs were taken of the corpses holding pistols.

'Last night,' a statement by the Minister of the Interior, Frédéric Duvigneaud read, 'in the interval of exactly one month from 29 July, the Forces of Order once again were faced with the old revolutionary demon and again triumphed. Charles and Ducasse Jumelle who, with their brother Clément Jumelle, were the co-authors of the Mahotières[4] and Pétionville bomb plots and the tragic events of 29 July, were killed last night...'

Subsequently the owner of the house in which the two brothers were found, Jean-Jacques Monfiston, was arrested and taken to Fort Dimanche where he was slowly tortured to death in an effort to extract information from him as to the whereabouts of Clément. But Monfiston remained silent until the end and Clément Jumelle eventually died of natural causes.

Nobody, or so it appeared, could oust Papa Doc Duvalier and on 30 April 1961 as if to prove this point, elections were held and duly rigged in order that he could win 100 per cent of the votes. An article in the *New York* Times ran as follows: 'Latin America has witnessed many fraudulent elections throughout its history but none has been more outrageous than the one which has just taken place in Haiti.'

Unperturbed by this and other comments from abroad, Duvalier declared that his party was the only legitimate and legal one in Haiti and duly appointed all fifty-eight congressional seats to Duvalierists.

It was at this juncture that the USA, who had up until then

supported the Duvalier regime[5] ceased its economic aid programme due to John F. Kennedy's increasing concern that Duvalier was misappropriating the money, siphoning it off into his own private bank accounts. Kennedy was also concerned that Duvalier wished to employ the US Marine Corps to strengthen the Tontons Macoute. However, the US's reluctance to support Papa Doc only served to strengthen his image at home, for it gave Duvalier the perfect excuse to portray himself as a principled opponent of a thuggish, uncaring America. Further attempts were then made at ousting Duvalier, supposedly with the covert backing of America's Central Intelligence Agency, but coup after coup came to nothing, and far from growing weaker in the face of opposition; Duvalier went from strength to strength. By 1964 the annual per capita income in Haiti was at an all-time low (in fact it was the lowest in the whole of the western hemisphere) standing at $80, added to which the illiteracy rate (despite a 'Duvalierist' campaign to eradicate it) still stood at 90 per cent. Haiti's population suffered food and fuel shortages, the latter causing blackouts all over the country. But none of the above concerned Duvalier, quite the contrary, for in April of that year he changed the Haitian constitution and had himself appointed president for life. On 4 March The *Haiti Journal* declared:

'Duvalier is the professor of energy. Like Napoleon Bonaparte, Duvalier is an electrifier of souls, a powerful multiplier of energy...Duvalier is one of the greatest leaders of contemporary times...because the Renovator of the Haitian Fatherland synthesizes all there is of courage, bravery, genius, diplomacy, patriotism, and tact in the titans of ancient and modern times.'

Of course, as with all dictators, there were hundreds of uncorroborated horror stories (the majority of which came from those fleeing Haiti) which might, or might not be true, but it is safe to say that even if one tenth were accurate then Duvalier's regime was one of the worst in world history. For instance, it is said that while victims were being tortured by the Tontons Macoute, Duvalier would watch from behind peepholes in the walls. There is also a story concerning six teenagers who, in an attempt at free expression, spray-painted a wall with the words, 'DOWN WITH DUVALIER'. Each of the teenagers, was hunted down and murdered after which Duvalier declared that all youth groups from that point on, would be illegal, adding that membership would also be punishable by death. Another story involves a political opponent of Duvalier's, Yvan D. Laraque, who was tracked down and killed in the north of the country. His body was shipped back to Port-au-Prince where it was dressed in underwear and propped up at an intersection between Grand' Rue and Somoza Avenue, under a Coke sign that read, 'WELCOME TO HAITI'. It rotted there in the sun for days on end. Laraque had been involved in yet another attempt to end Duvalier's reign of terror (this time near Jérémie airport) and afterwards the Tontons Macoute were ordered to kill the families of all those who had fought alongside him. According to several accounts men, women and children were tortured and executed and one family in particular was singled out for reprisals, the Sansaricqs. They were made to walk naked through the streets of Jérémie before they were shot dead. It was also reported that the Tontons Macoute initiated the practice of shooting women and children first to further enrage and upset the male members of their families and that often children were hacked to death whilst still being carried in their mothers' arms.

Nor did the insanity end there. Another bizarre, though less bloodcurdling act was a project to build a utopian city. To this end, the populace, together with any foreigners who had a financial interest in Haiti, were fleeced of their money, all of which went into building Duvalierville (now known as Cabaret) which was erected in honour of Papa Doc. It was filled not only with statues and monuments of the president, but also with enormous neon signs proclaiming, 'I HAVE NO ENEMIES SAVE THE ENEMIES OF HAITI' or 'I AM THE BEST THING THAT HAS EVER HAPPENED TO YOU.'

But perhaps the most extraordinary piece of self-promotion came when the government printed a booklet called *Le Catéchisme de la revolution* which contained a revised Lord's Prayer:

'Our Doc who art in the National Palace for life, hallowed

be Thy name by present and future generations. Thy will be done at Port-au-Prince and in the provinces. Give us this day our new Haiti and never forgive the trespasses of the anti-patriots who spit ever day on our country; let them succumb to temptation, and under the weight of their venom, deliver them not from any evil…'

Two of these 'anti-patriots', Marcel Numa and Louis Drouin, were involved in yet another attempted overthrow of Duvalier (there had been eleven other attempts) and were subsequently caught. On 12 November 1964 they were tied to pine poles and set before a nine-man firing squad. Crowds were encouraged to attend the execution, men, women and children, and leaflets were handed out in support of Papa Doc, who, it was said, would always protect the people of Haiti from such renegades. The whole event was then televised and broadcast to the entire nation as if it were some kind of game show.

Added to this there were also rumours of black magic ceremonies being held in the presidential palace. Several former associates of Duvalier reported that Papa Doc studied goat's entrails for political guidance; that one night a year he would sleep on the gravestone of General Dessalines with whom he claimed he was in spiritual contact; that he was constantly summoning sorcerers (*bocors*) to the palace to help him see into the future; that he buried people alive and had his Voodoo associates sacrifice babies in his honour.

All of the above served only to create misery and fear throughout the populace, added to which the appalling average national wage meant that intellectuals, teachers, doctors, college-educated professionals, all began leaving Haiti in droves. It was too dangerous for them to stay, let alone the fact that they could barely scrape together a living. A serious lack of medical supplies and malnutrition bordering on famine swept the island. The majority of the population were living a borderline existence in huts without sanitation or clean running water. Even when, after John F. Kennedy's untimely death in 1963, the US relaxed its stance on Haiti (once again because of its strategic location near Cuba) and began sending in aid, the people weren't helped because, true to form, Duvalier misappropriated the funds and transferred them into his own secret bank accounts.

By 1967, attempts to oust Papa Doc from power had intensified. Several bombs exploded near the presidential palace after which nineteen of Duvalier's presidential guards (including Major Jose Borges who had been in charge of the Radio 'Voice of the Duvalierist Revolution') were arrested, executed and buried at Fort Dimanche.

'I am an arm of steel,' said Duvalier after this latest blood was spilt, 'hitting inexorably...hitting inexorably...hitting inexorably. I have shot these...officers in order to project the revolution and those serving it...I align myself with great leaders of peoples as Kemal Ataturk, Lenin, Kwame Nkrumah, Patrice Lumumba, Azikwe, Mao Tse-tung.'

Other coups followed, including several begun overseas by disenfranchised exiles.In fact it wasn't until 1971 that Haiti saw an end to their dictator's rule. Having suffered months of ill health, suddenly on 22 April, François 'Papa Doc' Duvalier died (doctors diagnosed myocardial infarcts) and for a brief moment the entire country, save for his family and a few loyal followers, heaved a sigh of relief. His funeral, which was held two days later lasted six hours during which 101 rounds of cannon fire were let off, while a Haitian musician sang a composition entitled, 'Françoise, we thank you for loving us. Your star will be shining in the night'.

But the mild euphoria that the populace experienced at Papa Doc's departure was soon deadened, for back in the early sixties, when Duvalier rigged the election in his favour, he had also changed the constitution so that his son, Jean-Claude, could take over the reins of power on his death. Much like another, later dictator, Saddam Hussein, François Duvalier was all set to establish a tyrannical dynasty, only he hadn't counted on 'Baby Doc's complete inadequacy.

Initially, it looked as if Baby Doc might be different from his father, a kinder, more lenient leader. For instance, on coming to power he introduced several economic and judicial reforms, reopened the same military academy that his father had closed, whilst also releasing some political prisoners. But the words 'like father, like son' couldn't be better applied when talking about the Duvaliers, for Baby Doc, while declaring an amnesty for all exiles, simultaneously excluded all Communists and troublemakers from returning. In effect, this meant the majority of exiles still had to remain outside the country. Baby Doc also refused to allow any opposition to his presidency and insisted on retaining ultimate control over whom he appointed within government. In addition, US agents reported that huge amounts (in the region of 64 per cent) of Haiti's revenues were being skimmed off and misappropriated, together with tens of millions of dollars from public funds which all ended up in Baby Doc's Swiss bank accounts.

The Baby Doc years were just as turbulent and unpleasant, if not more so, than the Papa Doc years for the majority of Haitians. Despite causing as much social unrest as they could without endangering their lives, they had to suffer further years of misrule. Finally on 7 February1986, with the military pressing for his abdication, Baby Doc and his wife accepted an offer of assistance from the US government and fled into self-imposed exile in France.

With the Duvaliers gone, it might have been hoped that their hold over Haiti would soon be forgotten, but for a country where the majority of people still believe in and practice Voodoo, the influence of the dead over the living is so entrenched that no doubt somewhere, someone is still praising their 'Papa', still fearful that his spirit might return.

POL POT

ARCHITECT OF GENOCIDE

The red, red blood splatters the cities and plains of
the Cambodian fatherland,
The sublime blood of the workers and peasants,
The blood of revolutionary combatants of both sexes,
The blood spills out into great indignation and a resolute
urge to fight.
17 April, that day under the revolutionary flag,
The blood certainly liberates us from slavery.

NATIONAL ANTHEM OF DEMOCRATIC KAMPUCHEA

In 1998, the world watched in disbelief as footage was released of an old man who had died in the jungles of Thailand. He had a broad, chubby face with sparkling, grandfatherly eyes and thick lips that split into a toothy, genial grin. He looked slightly comical, an impression not dispelled by his peculiar name, Pol Pot. But there was nothing funny about Pol Pot – he was a leader who showed his people no mercy. On the run since 1979, this was the one-time ruler of Cambodia who was responsible for the deaths of almost two million people, a third of Cambodia's population. Over a period of four years, he had tortured and starved the Cambodians to death and men, women, children and babies were often brutally clubbed with hammers and buried alive.

Born Saloth Sar, in 1925, the youngest of seven children, he was brought up on a prosperous rice farm north of Phnom Penh, in a Cambodia ruled by the French. The young boy never worked in a rice field, or knew much about village life because at the age of six he was sent to the capital to train as a monk. He spent six years in a Buddhist temple and two years as a Buddhist monk. But the boy from the village only felt like an outsider in the bustling, modern city. Pol Pot didn't have a sense of the multi-cultural nature of the Cambodian cities, or if he did, he resented it. He said he felt, 'like a dark monkey from the mountains.'

In 1949, Pol Pot went to Paris as a student when he was awarded a scholarship to study Radioelectricity. Here he met his first wife, Khieu Ponnary, eight years his senior and the first Cambodian woman to be awarded the Baccalaureate. There his innate racism would find expression in extreme communism. During the years that Pol Pot studied in Paris, the Communist Party was probably the most hard-line, doctrine-led Stalinist Party in western Europe. He also absorbed the philosophy of another left-wing Cambodian student, Khieu Samphan, who believed that to achieve a true, rural revolution Cambodia needed to regress to a peasant economy – without towns, industry, currency or education.

After university in Paris, Pol Pot returned to Cambodia full of revolutionary ideals, and joined the underground Communist Party in opposition to the French-backed monarch, King Sihanouk and President Lon Nol. Within two years he was made General Secretary of the Party, and in order to escape capture by government forces, he fled to the hills, with his now heavily armed cadres, and preached his revolutionary doctrine to the hill tribes whilst also waging a vicious guerrilla war. Even then, Pol Pot had his sights on ultimate power and in 1962 it is believed that he ordered the execution of his predecessor as leader of the Communist Party. Initially, he was extremely unpopular with the peasants, but that would all change once he was in power.

From the early 1970s, Pol Pot and his group, known as the Khmer Rouge, engaged in a savage campaign against the Lon Nol government, and by 1972 the conflict had escalated into a full-blown civil war. Pol Pot's ruthless march to power was also boosted when the Vietnam War spilled over into Cambodia. The massive American bombardments that fell on the Cambodian people between 1969-1973 supplied Pol Pot with a potent hate-object and undoubtedly delivered to the revolution thousands of recruits and sympathizers. In 1970 the Party had 4,000 members; by 1975 they had 14,000. Between 1970-75 the Americans had supplied $1.18 billion in military material, and an additional $503 million in assistance, to Lon Nol's Khmer Republic. Then, suddenly America stopped all aid to Cambodia, which sent the country into a period of economic and military destabilization. Pol Pot took advantage of the government's weakness and by the spring of 1975, the Khmer Rouge was on the outskirts of Phnom Penh.

On 17 April, just after the Cambodian New Year, the Khmer Rouge entered the capital, victors of a five-year war against a government backed by the Americans. When it was announced that Pol Pot, a rubber plantation worker, was the new Prime Minister, no one had ever heard of him. It wasn't until 1978, when his picture began to appear in communal dining halls, that his own brothers and sisters realized that it was their brother who was in charge of the government.

After twenty-four years in existence, the Communist Party of Cambodia, now renamed Kampuchea had won a stunning victory. As a political force it had been almost totally unknown five years earlier, when Prince Sihanouk, Cambodia's king, had been overthrown. Now Pol Pot's regime was in a position to put in place and carry out an extreme, pure, total revolution of a sort that was more complete than any other revolution in history. The outside world reacted with amazement when the revolutionaries emptied the cities, destroyed western consumer goods, abolished money and foreign exchange markets. They established state control over all domestic and foreign trade, and then began liquidating the westernized elite.

The Central bank was demolished with explosives and bank notes allowed to flutter through the deserted streets of the capital. The Roman Catholic cathedral in Phnom Penh was disassembled stone by stone, until no trace whatever remained of the most prominent western edifice in the country.

Flushed with victory and imbued with a sense of righteousness, Pol Pot set out to implement his plans to restructure Cambodian society. The plan was to erase everything that had gone before and start again, even to the point that they declared that the year was no longer 1975, but Year Zero. This was to be the beginning of four years of murder and misery for the Cambodian people as Pol Pot began to destroy and rip apart Cambodian society, reducing it to a state of barbarity. The Khmer revolution altered completely and immediately the most basic aspects of Cambodian life such as language, religion and work habits.

Within hours of entering Phnom Penh, the new authorities ordered the city to be evacuated. Initially, they claimed this was to ensure that everyone got enough to eat, since the countryside had more food, and to ensure victory over the concept of private property, which was banned under the new regime. In reality it was because the new government could not control the towns, as their supporters were, by and large illiterate peasants, and the cities were considered to be centres of foreign domination.

Whether a doctor, lawyer, teacher, mechanic or street sweeper, everyone was forced into the countryside to labour as a peasant, where they would grow rice and build dams for the revolution. Two million Cambodians living in Phnom Penh were evacuated in seventy-two hours; soldiers marched from door to door and literally shoved people out onto the streets at gunpoint – if they resisted they were shot on the spot. The forced march of approximately three million out of Phnom Penh, and hundreds of thousands of others from Cambodia's provincial towns, meant death for around 400,000 people from heat, lack of food and water and, not least, the total absence of any medical assistance. 'From noon onwards, the masses in the streets multiplied as Communist troops uprooted more and more families…there was a huge crowd of every age and condition, young, old and sick…virtually everybody saw corpses rapidly bloating and rotting in the sun. Then the water supply ceased throughout the city…No stores of drinking water, no stocks of food, no shelter had been prepared for the millions of outcasts. Acute dysentery racked and sapped life from bodies already weakened by hunger and fatigue, we must have passed the body of a child every two hundred yards.'

Through the forced evacuation of the cities, the Khmer Rouge had virtually cut off the entire population from whatever material connection it had with the old order. All homes, money, bank accounts and consumer goods were left behind. Potential adversaries were disorganized and separated from the places that might serve as centres of resistance, making Pol Pot's regime total masters. Familiar social, religious, familial and economic patterns were shattered, as all evacuees were thrown into a basic struggle for survival.

To reinforce his policies, Pol Pot declared that, henceforth, the Buddhist religion, money and personal possessions would all be banned. It was back to basics. Believing the city people to be contaminated by past lives, Pol Pot would rewrite their histories. In the idealized peasant state, they would be purified through hard labour and brutality. Elderly monks who had not done manual labour for decades were forced to do particularly punishing work, digging for very long hours. People – including pregnant women – stood in water up to their necks in the cold and rainy seasons, working on canals, with legs and feet swelling up and bleeding. If you stopped work because of illness, you did not get fed. The Khmer Rouge slogan at the time was, 'to keep you is no gain and to destroy you is no loss.' Everyone laboured in the same way. If you didn't – you were shot. Fear and the threat of arbitrary, casual death was everywhere.

Pol Pot believed that for his vision of purity to work, individualism had to be obliterated. Only by destroying every root, every vestige of individual thought would a people dedicated to a collectivist regime emerge. With this in mind the population was divided into three categories, depending on class background and political past. Penh sith, who had full rights; triem, those who were candidates for full rights; and those who had no rights whatsoever, bannheu. The penh sith received full food rations and were allowed to join any organization, including the Party and the army. Almost all of them had joined Pol Pot at an early stage and came from the poorest, most uneducated segments of the rural population. Triems were second in line for rice rations and allowed to hold minor political offices. Many of these were drawn from the rural population, but as time went on some of the poor who had been forced out of the cities were promoted to this status. The lowest category, the Bannheu, had no rights whatever, not even the right to food. Most individuals targeted for liquidation fell into this category. Those not immediately executed received a near-starvation diet and were expected to work to the point of exhaustion.

With the advent of the new revolutionary morality, husbands were separated from wives for long periods, permission to marry was only granted by Angkar (The Organization), and that was within strict guidelines, and premarital sex became subject to extreme punishment, sometimes even the death penalty. Drinking and gambling were banned, and by 1976 Khieu Samphan, an officer of Angkar declared that, 'there were no thieves, drunkards, hooligans, or prostitutes in our country.' Angkar also considered itself to be the parents of all Cambodian children. Young teenagers were taken away from their families and sent away for rigorous ideological training. Pol Pot believed that if they trained their young recruits on cruel games, they would end up as soldiers with a love of killing, and encouraged the young recruits to take pleasure in tormenting animals and to make their victims suffer as much as possible.

Children scarcely lived with their parents any more: those under the age of six were entrusted to 'grandmothers' who cultivated their revolutionary spirit through the narration of heroic tales. Between the ages of six and twelve the children lived in separate quarters and were encouraged to spy and report on their parents for any infractions of the rules. Once they were twelve, they were enlisted in 'mobile troops' and hardly ever had the opportunity to see their parents again. In Pol Pot's hands they were taught nothing but discipline – just to take orders and not to look for reasons.

Pol Pot was now head of the ironically named Democratic Kampuchea and would brook no opposition to his plans to restructure society. The Sangha, the Buddhist monkhood, the only remaining institution that might have challenged Pol Pot by representing the traditional Cambodia, was ill prepared to resist the totalitarian power of the Khmer Rouge, and was dismantled. Before Pol Pot took power, Cambodia was considered to be the most Buddhist country in South East Asia. The countryside was dotted with more than 2,500 temples, and most men became monks at some point in their lives. Immediately after victory however, the Khmer Rouge moved swiftly to expunge all vestiges of Buddhism from daily life, since its teachings and practices contradicted vital aspects of the revolutionary doctrine. They executed the leading monks, defrocked the rest, forbade the accumulation of merit through giving, and destroyed many of the temples.

The Khmer Rouge then began to identify and execute political leaders, military officers, civil servants and anyone with an education. In some instances the spouses and children of the officials were killed alongside the supposed traitors. 'The Khmer Rouge thrust each official forward and stabbed them in the chest and back. As each man lay dying, his anguished and horror-stricken wives and children were herded up to his body. The women, forced to kneel, were stabbed to death and the children were stabbed where they stood. The very small children, too young to fully appreciate what was happening, were picked up by the executioners and torn limb from limb.'

King Sihanouk was discredited and put under virtual house arrest. Pol Pot was embarking on a policy of permanent purge that strove to create a society with no past and no alternatives.

According to eye-witnesses, much of the slaughter was carried out by fanatical brain-washed teenagers in red bandanas, who screamed and fired into the air while selecting their next victims. The youthful murderers were illiterate and ignorant and this made them even more violent and unpredictable. The killing was indiscriminate; the Khmer Rouge didn't need reasons. Whenever Pol Pot's troops were faced with a lack of comprehension or passive resistance, they chose to exterminate rather than take the time and trouble to re-educate.

Schools and libraries had been closed shortly after the Khmer Rouge came to power and newspapers were non-existent. The wearing of spectacles was enough to identify you as a member of the intelligentsia and therefore an enemy of the revolution. Everyone ate communally and individuals were only allowed to have two basic possessions of their own: a spoon and a bowl. Once ordinary shoes wore out, footwear consisted of Ho Chin Min sandals, improvised from pieces of rubber tyres and they were allowed one piece of clothing, a black boiler suit. All foreign medical supplies ceased in 1975 and the new government promoted the use of medicinal compounds made from local herbs. Untrained personnel performed medical operations. Even when disease ravaged the land throughout most of 1975 and 1976 Pol Pot remained inflexible – he repeatedly reminded people of the vital importance of self-reliance. If the bullet didn't get you, starvation would.

South East Asia is dominated by its staple food, rice. The average person would consume the equivalent of seven cans of rice per day. People who laboured in the rice paddies for up to fifteen hours a day, had to exist on one-and-a-half cans. Pol Pot expected rice production to treble in the first three years of his regime, believing that enthusiasm and heroism would be enough. But disastrous harvests as a result of the increased population in the countryside, and the urban people's inability to farm meant starvation. However, the Khmer Rouge refused to back down and constantly overstated its achievements. Life wasn't even cheap; it had no value at all. Cambodia became a macabre network of killing fields. Even today, the exact number of mass graves into which the victims' bodies were thrown, is not known.

Pol Pot also imposed a rigid organization plan that outlined when planting, weeding and harvesting was to occur, despite the fact that the country's conditions varied from place to place. There was no incentive in the propertyless society; you worked to avoid getting killed and even in death, one's body might be used as fertiliser. A phrase evolved for those executed: 'to be turned into a coconut'. Life became a continuous process of working in the rice fields during part of the year and on the irrigation systems during the remainder, with no respite in-between. If a worker made a mistake or criticized a project, they were taken away to be flogged to death or shot. Special offenders, like those starving peasants found cannibalising dead bodies, would be buried up to their heads in the ground and left to die. Their heads would then be cut off and stuck on stakes as a warning to others.

Within two years of Pol Pot coming to power, hundreds of thousands of Cambodians lay rotting in mass graves. Summary executions, starvation and overwork had taken its toll on both the city people and the peasants. The architect of this misery controlled every aspect of people's lives, but he never accepted that he was responsible for any of their suffering, or that anyone who died did so for anything but the right reason. Terror was the chief instrument of Pol Pot's dictatorship which sought to liquidate, as quickly as possible, all officers and many enlisted men in Lon Nol's army, bureaucrats of the old regime, landowners, those engaged in commerce, skilled labourers, western-educated professionals and many Buddhist monks.

The truly extraordinary aspect of the Pol Pot revolution was the literalism with which they applied abstract political principles, without regard for the awesome costs to Cambodia in terms of diplomatic isolation, economic devastation and massive human suffering. Other revolutionaries have talked long and loud on the subject, but have always been sobered by the responsibilities of power. The scope and extreme literalism with which Pol Pot pursued his aims of complete sovereignty and self-reliance make him unique. The Khmer Rouge leaders had been living in their own peculiar dream world, in which the human element was virtually forgotten. What they saw as a rational economic organization may have made sense in the isolation of the forest, but as an operative policy, it was cruel and unrealistic.

With the country closed to outsiders, the world was blissfully unaware of what was happening – or chose to ignore it for reasons of political expediency. Refugees reaching neighbouring countries told stories of unbelievable horrors. Yet with no diplomatic ties, no travel, not even a postal service, the nation of Kampuchea was an impenetrable armed camp, seemingly set on the genocide of its own people. When the United Nations called for a debate, Pol Pot's ministers sent their regrets that they could find no one with the time to spare to attend the hearings.

But two journalists, (one of them Elizabeth Becker) did get into Cambodia in 1978. Accompanied by the British academic, Malcolm Caldwell, they met Pol Pot, and he then proceeded to give them a lecture on the wonders of his experiments in Kampuchea. Later that night, an unremarkable meeting with Pol Pot turned into a unforgettable nightmare. Hearing gunfire coming from Malcolm Caldwell's room, Elizabeth rushed upstairs and found his body riddled with bullet holes. She still cannot work out why he died and not her.

Whilst propaganda films projected a country in the grip of well-being, Pol Pot had exterminated the majority of his class enemies and broken the old system. He now turned his attention to enemies within his own government. When Pol Pot took over in 1975, there were twenty-two members of the central committee of the Communist Party. By the end of his reign – three years, eight months and twenty days later – eighteen of those twenty-two had been executed. Murder by government under Khmer Rouge rule was so systematic that a large bureaucracy was required to eliminate the projected, suspected and imagined opponents of the transformation of Kampuchean society. The nerve centre of the purge apparatus was the Santebal, or special branch.

In a former school house in Phnom Penh, Pol Pot established the notorious Tuol Sleng prison or S-21, as an extermination centre at the hub of a nationwide system of imprisonment, interrogation, torture and execution. Initially set up for the interrogation of counter-revolutionaries, over 20,000 people were tortured and executed here on trumped-up charges of spying for the KGB or the CIA – or simply because they knew someone who had been arrested before. Men, women and children were tagged and almost all were tortured into confessing anything they were told to confess. Of the 4,000 who entered S-21, only 7 survived and 1 was released – the rest were buried in S-21's customized killing field, Cheung Ek, where over 8,000 skulls have so far been counted.

Anyone brought into S-21 was photographed and their crimes were meticulously recorded. The Khmer Rouge had developed their own code for recording the crimes and fates of the prisoners. At any one time, the prison held around 1,500 prisoners. The ideology of the prison was that the Party was never, ever wrong. If people were arrested they were guilty – indeed the word for prisoner in Cambodian means guilty person, rather than somebody who is being held.

A tiny rectangular notebook found in a house near Tuol Sleng contains five hand-written pages on Human Experiments on seventeen different prisoners. Deuch, the governor of S-21, recorded the effects of slashing a girl's stomach and placing her in water to see how long she would float. Similar details were recorded for, 'four young girls stabbed in the throat.' One of the problems that repeatedly emerged from the files left behind was that torture became too indiscriminate and prisoners were dying before information could be extracted from them. This represented a 'loss of mastery'.

With class and political opponents out of the way, Pol Pot, compelled by the racism that was so much a part of his agenda, now turned his attention to Cambodia's ethnic minorities. Pol Pot believed there was only one pure race: the Khmer, who originated in Lower Cambodia. The Chinese were probably the largest ethnic minority in Cambodia and half of them perished in the Pol Pot regime. The Ethnic Chams and Muslims were directly targeted and ruthlessly slaughtered. But Pol Pot's most extreme persecution was reserved for the Kampuchean Vietnamese. The Khmer Rouge had been eliminating the Vietnamese in Kampuchea since 1970 but now it became a crime punishable by death to speak or look Vietnamese. Kampuchean men married to Vietnamese women were instructed to kill their wives or else face execution themselves. In excess of 20,000 ethnic Vietnamese lost their lives. Even Pol Pot's Northern Zone Secretary, Kang Chap was ordered to shoot his wife because she was half-Vietnamese. He did as he was ordered.

The Khmer Rouge publicly glorified revolutionary violence and blood sacrifice and celebrated them in the country's official documents. The blood spilt for the revolution became a sanctifying symbol. Virtually every line of the national anthem mentioned bloodshed. It was as if the revolutionaries were harnessing the darker, more violent side of their national character to give their own deplorable acts legitimacy.

By late 1978, with executions and starvation at their height, and with the Pol Pot regime seemingly invincible, the government began to self-destruct. With information only coming from its security forces, the Party fell under the spell of the counterespionage myth, consuming itself as it nearly consumed the people of Cambodia. No traditional institutions existed to check the Party authority. They had crushed any opposition by terror and coercion. Now Pol Pot's psychotic and life-long hatred for the Vietnamese would be his undoing.

After a series of violent border confrontations with Vietnam, 150,000 Vietnamese troops stormed across the Kampuchean border and by 6 January, they were approaching Phnom Penh. Pol Pot's repeated purges had broken the links of command between officers and men and shattered morale in both the army and Party. Those targeted as traitors who knew they were not, did not know what to do; die in the name of the Party or flee. However the Cambodian people themselves knew what to do – they welcomed the Vietnamese with open arms and shouts of joy. Ironically three Vietnamese Cambodians, who had escaped the purge, Heng Samrin, Chea Sim and Ros Samay, would soon head the government that replaced Pol Pot.

Pol Pot and his henchmen fled to Northern Cambodia and Thailand and the hated governor of S-21, Deuch, evaded capture by one hour. Forty-four months after capturing Phnom Penh the Khmer Rouge were swept from the capital by Vietnamese invasion forces. The intervening period had witnessed the greatest per capita loss of life in a single nation in the twentieth century. In the search for 'pure communism', the Khmer Rouge reduced a war-torn, but traditionally resilient, economy to one almost without prospect of spontaneous regeneration. The draconian rules of life according to Pol Pot had turned Cambodia into a nation-wide gulag.

As Pol Pot fled in a white Mercedes and helicopter, taking him and his aides to Thailand, thousands more Khmer Rouge cadres left a ravaged Cambodia. He continued to fight on from his power base among his dedicated followers in the countryside and formed the Khmer Peoples' Liberation Front announcing a hypocritical manifesto promising political and religious freedom. It would be another twenty years before Pol Pot was seen again – but this time he was on trial.

Finally the Khmer Rouge had turned against their former leader. They had arrested him, not for crimes of genocide or crimes against humanity, but for being a political enemy. In an interview conducted by Nate Thayer shortly before his death, Pol Pot refused to say whether he regretted having caused the deaths of so many innocent people, and said that the mistakes made by the regime were mainly in implementation of policy. Two weeks later, in April 1998 Pol Pot died of natural causes.

Five years after his death, Pol Pot's comrades in slaughter have still not been brought to trial. Mass grave sites have been discovered throughout Cambodia, mainly in remote areas. Skulls have been collected and piled into an enclosure to serve as a reminder of Pol Pot's evil. Evidence is still being collected for a United Nations-backed tribunal, but progress is being hampered by the fact that Khmer Rouge operatives occupy posts in the new Cambodian government. When Cambodia's foreign minister, Ieng Sary, finally admitted to the deaths of three million people during the Khmer Rouge regime, he claimed that Pol Pot had been misunderstood and the massacres had all been 'a mistake'.

IDI AMIN

THE BUTCHER OF EAST AFRICA

*His Excellency President for Life Field Marshal Al Hadji Dr
Idi Amin, VC, DSO, MC, Lord of All the Beasts of the Earth
and Fishes of the Sea and Conqueror of the British Empire in
Africa in General and Uganda in Particular.*

TITLE AND STYLE ADOPTED BY IDI AMIN
AS PRESIDENT OF UGANDA

In 1971, the self-created General Idi Amin became President of
Uganda. To the rest of the world he was a showman whose
extravagance was exceeded only by his talent for comic
buffoonery. But behind the grinning face was a calculating
monster, who brought about a tragedy of monumental
proportions. He set up the notorious State Research Bureau,
which, on his orders, slaughtered thousands of innocent
Ugandans in a campaign of ethnic cleansing, and executed his
enemies live on television. He mutilated his wife and murdered
his ministers, keeping the head of one in his refrigerator as a
warning to others. By the end of his reign, over 300,000 people,
one in sixty of his population, had been murdered.

Uganda is a landlocked country in East Africa. Covering a
total of just over 93,000 square miles, it is slightly smaller in size
than Great Britain. It is bordered by the Sudan to the north,
Kenya to the east, Tanzania and Rwanda to the south and the
Congo to the west. A former British colony, Uganda gained
independence on 9 October 1962. Under British rule, economic
power and education were concentrated in the south, whilst
the majority of the armed forces, police and paramilitary forces
were drawn from the north. This imbalance would help to
shape the savage history of Uganda.

Idi Amin Dada was born around 1928 in Uganda's West
Nile district. His father was a Kakwa Muslim and his mother a
Christian Lugbara, a neighbouring tribe of the Kakwa. Both

these tribes are generally defined as Nubians, renowned for their sadistic brutality, lack of formal education and ability to poison their enemies. His parents separated when Idi was very young and the young boy moved from one army barracks to another with his camp-follower mother, who was purported to be a witch.

After only two years of primary education, Amin joined the King's African Rifles in 1946 as an assistant cook. His service record shows that he was always in trouble. Despite this, he was the physical type that the British liked best in their ranks – he was six-feet-four-inches tall and uneducated, characteristics his officers believed would ensure bravery in battle whilst making him more amenable to orders. Rising quickly through the ranks, Captain Amin was sent to England in 1962, to undertake a Commanding Officers' course in Wiltshire, but he returned in 1964 having failed to complete it. He was then sent to Israel on parachute training – again he failed to finish his training, but the Israelis gave him his wings anyway. By 1966 Amin had returned to Uganda and become Deputy Commander of the Ugandan military – he was now an indispensable ally to any politician wanting to rule the country.

But even before his return to Uganda, it was reported that Amin had been exhibiting signs of sadism. As a corporal fighting the Mau Mau uprising in Kenya in the 1950s he was said to have made members of the Karamajong tribe place their genitals on the table. He threatened to cut them off with a machete. It was also said that early in 1962 he was directly responsible for the murders of innocent Turkana tribesmen. His behaviour was reported to Obote, then Prime Minister of Uganda, via the British Governor but Amin was one of only two black officers in the whole Ugandan army on the eve of independence, so the incident was apparently hushed up and Amin was promoted to Colonel. He had been saved by the political winds of change; it was an error that Obote would come to regret bitterly.

It was not long, however, before Amin was in trouble again, this time it was his greed that led him there. In 1966 he was investigated for corruption, when it was discovered that within a month, he had deposited £20,000 in his bank account – more than a Ugandan colonel could earn in a decade. Amin suceeded in having the charges dropped.

By 1966, the political situation in Uganda was becoming increasingly volatile. Milton Obote had become the country's first Prime Minister in 1962 and his first priority had been to forge some sort of unity among the fourteen million Ugandans who owed more allegiance to their tribal chiefs than to any government in Kampala. Obote, a professional lawyer, came from the minority Langi tribe and, mindful of this, he appointed the powerful ruler of the Buganda tribe, King Freddy, as President. The Buganda tribe, largely anglicized by colonial commissioners and missionaries, was the largest single ethnic group in Uganda. They considered themselves the elite. But in placating them, Obote earned the growing distrust of all the other tribes.

Obote began to limit the power of the President and Buganda tribesmen started agitating for Obote's overthrow. Realizing that he needed to pit some military muscle against them, he chose the new Deputy Commander of the army, Idi Amin to help him keep control of the country.

Amin's response to the call was both swift and energetic. Using a 122mm gun mounted on his personal jeep, he blew gaping holes in King Freddie's palace. The president, warned of the danger just before the attack, fled into hiding and eventually made his way to Britain, where he died in lonely exile.

For the next four years, Amin was the Prime Minister's trusted strong-arm, and Milton Obote was calm and relaxed when, in January 1971, he flew off to Singapore to attend a Commonwealth conference. However, on 25 January, Radio Uganda started playing martial music throughout the morning and at 3.45p.m. Wilfred Aswa, a warrant officer, (destined to die three years later at the hands of Amin) read an announcement stating the reasons for the military coup. Amin was not mentioned in the first broadcast, but thirty minutes later it was announced that he had been asked by the armed forces to take over the country. His first words were: 'I am not a politician but a professional soldier. I am therefore a man of few words.' But now he was Uganda's President he would not stop talking.

Initially there was great jubilation among many sections of the population at the birth of the new regime. Following his overnight coup, Amin promised to return the country to democracy. It was a lie. Many of those who welcomed him were to suffer later at his hands. Foreign newspapers, particularly in Britain, hailed the event as a new era in Uganda. Amin's first move was to pacify tribal enemies and buy valuable breathing space. He persuaded Bugandan tribal leaders that he had actually tipped off King Freddy, giving him time to flee to safety, and he organized for the deceased President's body to be flown back and buried with full ceremony.

Encouraged by adulation and euphoria, Amin and his henchmen embarked on a campaign of genocide against the tribes who had supported the previous government. He purged the army, killing the members of Obote's tribe and his supporters. The West Nilers and Nubians were filled with a desire for vengeance, and Amin fuelled their passion with his own paranoia and blood lust. Soldiers started appearing at universities. They would look at the names on the doors and take away women with certain names, principally Bugandans, but not only from that tribe – these women would be dragged, screaming out into the night. They were never seen again.

In March 1972, Amin announced a re-structuring of the army and began by ordering thirty-six army officers to report to Makindye prison in Kampala, the capital of Uganda, for training in internal security. Disgruntled, but seduced by the thought of forming part of a government of military men rather than politicians, the officers arrived at the prison. They were placed in the cell called Singapore – both the prison and that cell in particular would become a byword for terror and torture. Through a spy hole in the door, the prisoners next door watched a hideous scene unfold. Some of the officers were crawling, screaming in pain because their arms and legs had been broken. Military guards prodded them with bayonets and knives to hurry them up – splitting their stomachs open, cutting their throats or beheading them. The blood lay half-an-inch thick on the floor.

The former army Chief-of-Staff, Brigadier Suleiman Hussein, was arrested and taken to another prison where he was beaten to death with rifle butts. His head was severed and taken to Amin's palatial new home in Kampala, where the President preserved it in the freezer compartment of his refrigerator. In two widely separated army barracks, at Mbara and Jinja, the elite of the officer corps were lined up on the parade ground to take a salute from an armored column. The tanks swept across the square, swung into line abreast formation and crushed most of the officers to death. Those left alive were used for target practice. At another barracks, the remaining staff officers were herded into a briefing room for a lecture by Amin. As they saw his gleaming Mercedes sweep into the square, the doors were locked from the outside and grenades were lobbed through the windows.

Within five months, Amin had killed most of the trained, professional officers in his army. Yet news of these events was kept from the Ugandan people, who were simply told that a few disloyal officers had been court-martialed and executed. To make up the gaps in the ranks, Amin promoted fellow Kakwa tribesmen. Cooks and drivers, mess orderlies and wireless operators became majors and colonels overnight. During the greater part of 1971, the up-country areas, where the majority of killings took place, were sealed off from foreigners and those attempting to find out the truth, such as the American journalist, Nicholas Stroh, who soon fell victim to Amin's wrath.

Stroh and his colleague, Robert Siedle had been asking questions about the army massacres. At Mbara barracks they were granted an interview with the new commander, Major Juma Aiga, a former taxi driver who had gained an instant army commission. When their persistent questioning became too much, Major Aiga telephoned Amin. His reply was said to be a terse: 'Kill them.' Two days later Aiga was seen driving around Kampala in Stroh's Volkswagen. The two Americans were never seen again.

Amin had now broken the back of the Ugandan army and

decided to set off on his first foreign trip as head of government. The trip was seen as the act of a man of peace, anxious to consolidate the security of Uganda on the world stage, but the reality was very different, Amin was looking to buy weapons to further establish his reign of terror in Uganda.

His first visit in July 1972 was to Israel, where he met with the Prime Minister, Golda Meir, but apart from a vague offer to supply training for his troops he left empty-handed. Then Amin decided to give his old colonial masters a surprise. The first that anyone knew of his visit was when the pilot of his plane radioed to the control tower at Heathrow Airport, announcing his arrival. The Queen was in residence at the time, and she was prevailed upon to give a luncheon at Buckingham Palace. When the Queen asked Amin for his reason for visiting Britain, he replied it was to shop for size fourteen shoes.

At a meeting with Edward Heath, the Prime Minister, Amin was more frank about his intentions. He wanted guns, aeroplanes, and ammunition, but he had no money with which to buy them and he was turned away. Furious at being rejected by his supposed allies, Amin returned to Uganda.

Meanwhile in Uganda, Amin's rages were becoming legendary. One hot August night in 1972, dinner guests at Amin's palace, State House, were shocked and revolted when he left the table and returned with the frost-encrusted head of Brigadier Hussein. In a ranting fit of rage, Amin screamed abuse at the severed head, throwing cutlery at it, before ordering his guests to leave.

When Amin had seized power in 1971, Uganda was by far the most economically viable state in East Africa. There were no shortages of essential commodities and hunger and abject poverty were unknown. Tourism was booming and had almost replaced cotton as the prime foreign exchange earner. At the beginning of 1971, Uganda's foreign reserves stood at twenty million pounds sterling, but by the end of the year they had dwindled to three million. Within a year of Amin coming to power, Uganda was virtually bankrupt. The President's response was to order the Bank of Uganda to print millions of worthless banknotes to pump into the economy. All that remained of the reserves of US dollars were made available for his personal use.

In Kampala the price of a bar of soap rose to £6, two weeks wages for the average worker on the coffee plantations, which were among the country's few remaining economic resources. Temporary salvation was offered by one other extravagant dictator, Libya's Colonel Gadaffi, with whom Amin met on 13 February 1972. The price was one Amin was only too happy to pay for their newly-formed alliance. As Libyan money poured into Kampala to keep the country barely afloat, Amin kept his side of the bargain.

Amin declared he was now against the State of Israel and backed the Palestinian cause, and on 27 March 1972 he ordered that all Israelis had to leave Uganda. He claimed they had been intending to poison the Nile and kill all Arabs in Sudan and Egypt. In an interview with Arab Week he said that he would lead the Arab troops to conquer Israel. The contradiction that wearing Israeli paratrooper wings on his uniform presented when he was depicted on the new Ugandan currency later that year, was lost on Amin. Angered and hurt, the Israelis pulled out. The documents they took with them included one slim volume which would help to make history – the plans of Israel's last gift to Uganda – the new passenger terminal, control tower and runway layout for Entebbe Airport.

Amin, anxious to prove to Gadaffi that he was a worthy protégé, opened an office in Kampala for the Palestine Liberation Organization, with full diplomatic status. He declared his admiration for Adolf Hitler and drew up plans for a memorial to the Nazi dictator to be erected in the middle of Kampala. When, in 1972, Palestinian terrorists massacred the Israeli Olympic team in Munich, Amin sent a telegram to the United Nations stating that: 'Hitler and all German people knew that the Israelis are not people who are working in the interest of the people of the world and that is why they burnt over six million Jews alive with gas on the soil of Germany. The world should remember that the Palestinians, with the assistance of Germany, made the operation possible in the Olympic village.'

By August 1972 Amin was in deep trouble inside Uganda. The economy was under intense pressure because of excessive military spending and his claims that the hundreds of people who had disappeared, had been murdered or spirited away by Zionists and imperialists, were no longer believed. There were fewer jobs than ever and violence and murder had become institutionalized. The civilians were complaining and even the army personnel were looking to Amin for a solution. Amin needed a diversion, and he needed money – the Asian population in Uganda were to be his next victims.

The Asians had originally come to Uganda to construct the railway as indentured labourers. Thousands had stayed and more had joined them later. Britain had used them to establish and consolidate its rule as middlemen – political and economic – between themselves and the Africans. They owned and controlled approximately half of Uganda's wealth, and were the focus of much internal jealousy.

Some early indicators of the coming harassment of Uganda's Asian community had already surfaced during 1971. Amin had ordered a head count and started to accuse them of currency racketeering, smuggling and isolationism. In January 1972 he warned that any Asians holding political meetings would be summarily shot. Then on 5 August he dropped his bombshell. He gave the 80,000 Asians ninety days to leave Uganda, claiming the idea had come to him in a dream from God. The expulsion opened the way for the state to seize the Asian community's assets for Amin to dispose of as he saw fit. Amin had given his answer to the masses and the greed of his soldiers.

For the next three months, Amin's voice could be heard on Uganda radio, making a daily countdown to the deadline. Although most of the Asians had lived in Uganda for generations, forming the backbone of the nation's commerce, they now fled in terror leaving behind their houses, offices, shops and plantations.

The Asians were treated brutally as they left Uganda. Some were killed by Amin's marauding troops. At airports, border posts, railway stations and road blocks they were harassed, manhandled, robbed and raped. They were forced to leave all their property behind with their businesses. Amin gave away the choice businesses to his friends and cronies. Pharmacies and surgeries were handed over to motor mechanics from the infamous State Research Bureau; textile warehouses were given to Research Bureau telephone operators and army corporals. Within weeks the shops were deserted, their stocks sold and the shelves never filled again. Africans, with no retail experience, fixed the prices of expensive foreign shirts in Kampala shops according to their collar size, thinking that it was the price tag.

Amin knew that in expelling the Asians he was causing difficulties for Britain as the majority of Asians with British passports fled there. But he had not finished with Britain yet, and on 17 December, in a midnight radio and TV broadcast, Amin announced that he was taking all property belonging to British citizens in Uganda. The Ugandan government was to take over all the tea estates as well as Uganda Television and the British Metal Corporation. Any Briton remaining would be accused of spying and would have to suffer with the consequences.

But Amin was creating a monster that needed to be fed constantly. The infamous State Research Bureau was a state within a state, run by men who did not seem to possess the hearts and feelings of human beings. He bought their loyalty with lavish gifts of money and expensive luxuries like video recorders and whiskey, and clothes imported from London and Paris.

Once the Asian and British businesses had been given up, the men of the State Research Bureau wanted to be paid again. With no money or property left to meet their demands, Amin gave them the only asset he had left, the lives of his fellow Ugandans. It was the most bestial mass murder contract in history. Amin had given his followers the licence to kill for profit.

He knew the custom of Ugandans, their deep reverence for the last remains of dead relatives, and that they would spend every last Ugandan schilling, and part with everything of value to recover the body of a loved one for burial. In many of the tribes, 'body finders' will earn their rewards by tracking through the bush to find the corpse of a father or son who has died in some remote area. Now the State Research Bureau became both the killers and the body finders.

Cruising through the streets of Kampala in their imported cars, wearing their uniform of gaudy shirts and bell-bottom trousers, they openly arrested ordinary townspeople. And at their headquarters, only a few hundred yards from Amin's home, they ruthlessly butchered their victims.

One of Amin's ministers later compiled a list of the tortures that they inflicted. They are as follows:

Slow killing was common practice. A man would be shot in the arms, chest and legs and left to bleed to death.

There was a technique for cutting a victim's flesh and force-feeding it to him raw until he bled to death.

A man's flesh would be cut, roasted and he would be forced to eat it until he died.

Certain prisoners were kept in very deep and dark holes. These holes were filled with ice-cold water in which the prisoners were kept and tortured to death.

Sticking bayonets through prisoners' anuses or genitals.

Women were raped or had their reproductive organs set on fire whilst still alive.

As the corpses piled up in the basement cells of the three-storey building, other Research Bureau investigators were dispatched to inform grieving families that their loved ones had disappeared after being arrested and were feared dead. For a body-finding fee of £150, or every last possession the family owned, the state-sponsored murderers would drive the widows and weeping sons and daughters to a lush forest on the outskirts of Kampala.

Almost every gulley and bush concealed a dead body. Night after night as many as a hundred families made the trip. The bodies not reclaimed were thrown into Lake Victoria, useless assets written off as a business loss until they floated through the sluice gates of the Owens Fall Dam or the hydroelectric generators.

Power cuts in Kampala now became commonplace.

Visitors, arms salesmen and foreign diplomats in the two showpiece hotels would grumble loudly when cocktail bars were plunged into darkness and the elevators jammed between floors. But the uncomplaining residents of Kampala would leave the unlit streets and go home behind their barricaded doors. The drop in the voltage could only mean one thing – that the hydroelectric dam at Owen Falls, forty miles west of Kampala, was once again clogged with rotting corpses. Time after time the generators had to be shut down and the water inlets cleared of the day's toll of death, which usually numbered forty to fifty corpses. Despite constant boat patrols on Lake Victoria, the maintenance engineers couldn't hope to spot every dead body. Luckily for them they had allies: crocodiles who would scavenge, eating the evidence. But even these voracious creatures had become bloated and lazy.

By now, the executions by firing squad at the Research Bureau were becoming a problem. The neighbouring French embassy staff complained directly to Amin about the constant gunfire through the night. Amin, sinking ever deeper into depravity, discussed a solution with the head of the Bureau, Lieutenant Isacc Malyamungu.

Malyamungu, a gatekeeper at a textile factory before Amin made him a government official, was a notoriously sadistic killer. After executing the Mayor of the town of Masaka, he had paraded the badly mutilated man through the streets carrying his amputated genitals in his hands. Now he and Amin calmly came up with a solution to the problem of maintaining the horrendous flow of very profitable killings without the disturbing, continuous rattle of gunfire.

Each murder victim would be kept separately in the basement, while another prisoner was offered the promise of reprieve, if he would batter the solitary man to death with a sledgehammer. Terrified, and pleading for their lives, few prisoners were brave enough to refuse the offer. But once they had carried out their grisly deed, the roles were changed. The unwilling executioner, usually sobbing and demented, would be left alone. He would become the solitary man, while in the cell next door another Ugandan was being given the sledgehammer and the heartless promise of life if he would repeat the procedure.

Even Amin's own wives were not safe from his insane paranoia and rages. In March 1974 he decided to divorce three of his four wives. He accused them of meddling in his affairs and ordered them out of his home. Three months later, one of the young ex-wives, Kay, died in an apartment in Kampala as the result of a clumsy abortion attempt. She had been four months pregnant. Amin, in a state of fury, rushed to the mortuary to see her body. Shortly afterwards, having barked a few orders at the hospital staff, he left.

Two hours later he returned and satisfied himself that his orders had been carried out. His youngest wife, Sarah, and Kay's young son, Aliga Amin, accompanied him. 'Pay close attention to what you see', he roared, 'Kay was a wicked woman and you must see what has become of her.' His ex-wife's mutilated torso lay on the operating table. Her head and all of her limbs had been amputated and her head had been reversed and sewn onto her torso face-down. Her legs had been sewn onto her shoulders and her arms attached to her bloodstained pelvis.

But Amin was about to suffer a huge embarrassment. On 28 June 1976, an Air France airliner, hijacked by a group of Palestinians, arrived at Entebbe Airport. The plane had been *en route* from Tel Aviv to Paris when it had been taken over near Athens. It carried some 300 passengers, most of whom were Jewish.

In the heart of an African country governed by a Hitler-worshipper, the hostages far from any hope of rescue, the Palestinians confidently drew up a list of demands while Amin looked on, gloating and basking in the world's limelight. Amin helped to draft the blackmailers' demands, stating that all the passengers would be killed within forty-eight hours, if fifty-three imprisoned Palestinians in Israel and Europe were not released. As international tension mounted, the deadline was extended until the early hours of 4 July, and non-Jewish passengers were allowed to leave.

Two days before the deadline, as terrified hostages huddled

together in the passenger terminal, one elderly Londoner, Dora Bloch, who held dual British-Israeli nationality, choked on a piece of food and was driven the twenty miles to hospital in Kampala. But as Idi Amin was being seen world-wide on television, badgering the hostages in the passenger lounge, Israeli engineers pored over the vital blueprints of the airport they had helped to build.

Shortly after midnight on 3 July, a task force of Israeli Air Force planes, filled with commandos, swept down over Lake Victoria and landed at Entebbe Airport. They taxied to the precise spot where the hostages were being held. In less than one hour they took off again with the rescued hostages, killing twenty of Amin's troops and all seven hijackers. They also took with them the bodies of two of their own men who had been caught in the crossfire.

But elderly Dora Bloch remained behind in Kampala Hospital, frail and barely able to breath – Amin decided to vent his fury on her. After she had received reassurance from the British High Commissioner, Peter Chandley, two of Amin's henchmen from the State Research Bureau crashed through the doors of the hospital. They pistol-whipped the frail widow and dragged her down three flights of stairs. Half-an-hour later they dumped her bullet-riddled body in a field on the outskirts of Kampala. When the High Commissioner went to see her, Amin informed him that she had been returned to the airport before the raid had taken place and was therefore with the other rescued passengers – a palpable lie since the commissioner had seen Mrs. Bloch after the raid had taken place.

And so the situation drifted on until the late 1970s. Amin assassinated the Anglican Archbishop, Janani Luwum and this was followed by the banning of all twenty-six Christian organizations working in Uganda. There was now an unprecedented out-pouring of exiles of every ethnic and political background. Amin received worldwide condemnation, even from those who had hitherto been his allies, and America's House of Representatives passed a resolution condemning his gross violation of human rights.

However, Amin remained undeterred, and people began to believe that their President was indestructible. It seemed as if their prayers were not being heard, and that God had forgotten the ill-fated people of Uganda.

But Amin was still vulnerable – especially from his own army. He could never totally eliminate those against him, in addition to which, other forces were now coming into play. Civilian subversive groups were forming and troops were preparing in Kenya and Tanzania. Amin's excesses had galvanized the opposition, especially the exiles living abroad.

Idi Amin's last desperate gamble to hold on to the reins of power collapsed in April 1979. In a moment of over-confidence bordering on insanity, and to scare the Ugandan people into submission, he claimed that the country was threatened by bloody invasion from its southern neighbour, Tanzania.

To give substance to his fantasies, Amin ordered small contingents of his troops to cross over to Tanzania on raids against the 'invaders'. Such provocation was too much for the Tanzanian President, Julius Nyrere. His soldiers repelled the attacks and then pressed on deep into Uganda. They were welcomed with open arms by the long-suffering Ugandans as they advanced towards Kampala, arriving in April 1979.

In his final television broadcast, Amin urged his troops to join him in a last stand at the town of Jinja. The soldiers never turned up, but then again neither did Idi Amin. He had fled in his personal aircraft to the safety of Libya to seek sanctuary with his one remaining ally, Colonel Gadaffi. The brutal reign of Idi Amin was over and today he lives near Mecca, in Saudi Arabia, a guest of the royal family.

SADDAM HUSSEIN

A STALIN OF THE MIDDLE EAST

'To those who know him personally, Saddam has no sense of humor and no patience for advice on diplomacy or image-building. He alternates his image between that of a father figure and tyrant.'

NORA BOUSTANY, THE *WASHINGTON POST*, 12 AUGUST 1990

If, for the past ten to twenty years, one man has acted as a thorn in the side of America then surely that man would be the President of Iraq, Saddam Hussein. During the 1980-88 Iran-Iraq war he ordered the use of chemical weapons against the Iranian forces, (killing between 450,000-730,000) and against Iraq's huge Kurdish population (killing between 150,000-340,000). More recently, Saddam Hussein's crimes have included the invasion of Kuwait (1990-91) killing over 1,000 of that country's citizens and in 1991 the suppression of both Kurdish and Shia insurgencies killing between 30,000-60,000 people. Further to this, he also ordered the destruction of southern Iraq's marshlands to prevent the marsh Arabs claiming a homeland and in 2003, after repeated calls by the US and its allies to relinquish all weapons of mass destruction, led his people into a second war with the West. That Saddam Hussein is a terrifying despot is not in doubt, but what made him into such a figure, a man so reviled by the West that aside from Hitler and Stalin, he alone stands as the most hated political figure of the twentieth century.

Saddam Hussein was born on 28 April 1937[1] in the small Sunni Muslim[2] village of Al Awja, only a few miles east of the town of Tikrit. His mother was a formidable woman by the name of Subha Tulfah Al Musallat while his father was Hussein Al Majid, but by the time of Saddam's birth, his father had disappeared and was presumed dead.

Saddam's childhood, while not impoverished in terms of

the type of society in which he lived, was still very humble. The family home was a one-room mud hut where the entire household, along with their animals, had to live and sleep. There would have been no sanitation to speak of, no electricity, no fresh water. In addition, the village of Al Awja, being situated in a particularly impoverished region of Iraq, offered little in the way of opportunities for a young boy.

'... Tikrit was known only for its watermelons and the skin boats called *kalaks* which carried them down the Tigris to Baghdad. Disease was rampant, in particular malaria, bilharzia and tapeworm. Most people suffered from one or more of these endemic maladies...While there are no records on the subject, life expectancy was very short.'[3]

Bearing the above in mind, it is not surprising to discover that the young Saddam spent most of his early years playing in Al Awja's back alleys, gaining a reputation as being a bit of a tearaway. Then, at the age of six, his mother remarried and his new stepfather put the young boy to work in the fields as a general farmhand. It was a tough life, made all the more tough by the abuse he suffered at the hands of his stepfather who refused to let him attend school. In fact, the only person Saddam looked up to or admired was a maternal uncle called Khairallah Tulfah. Tulfah was an educated man who had once been a second lieutenant in the Iraqi Army, after which he had become a schoolteacher.

In 1947, at the age of ten, Saddam Hussein left home to live with this much-loved relation. Indeed, according to various sources, the reason behind his sudden departure was because Saddam was not only desperate to gain an education and learn to read and write but wanted to find his way out of poverty and make his mark on the world.

Sometime between 1953-1954 Saddam took an entrance exam for the Baghdad Military College, but failed due to his lack of education. Coupled with his poverty-stricken peasant background, this setback no doubt added to an already substantial chip he had on his shoulder. Not withstanding this, however, he turned his mind towards politics. Saddam identified with the Sunni minority in Iraq, the poorest of the poor, and began participating in anti-government demonstrations. He persuaded gangs of thugs to join the cause and set them to beating up anyone who didn't agree with their anti-government stance. At the same time, Saddam also began making friends with more organized sections of the opposition, students who were affiliated with the Ba'ath, a political party that was founded in Syria around 1940.

On 14 July 1958, the Iraqi army, led by Brigadier Abdel Karim Kassem and Colonel Abdel Salam Aref, finally overthrew the Iraqi monarchy. Saddam couldn't have been better pleased if he'd perpetrated the act himself. This, or so he thought, would mark a new phase for his country, but by 1959 his attitude had changed so radically that on 7 October he attempted to assassinate Kassem (who had since taken over the presidency). Afterwards, realising the plot had failed, Saddam fled to Egypt, only returning to Iraq in 1963 when the Ba'ath party, led by Ahmad Hassan Al Bakr, staged a successful coup and finally overthrew Kassem. However, as is the way with Middle Eastern politics, and with Iraq in particular, nothing stayed settled for long and within months of arriving back in Iraq, Saddam was once again jailed after Colonel Abd-al-Salam Muhammad Aref seized power from the Ba'athists. Saddam eventually escaped and later, in 1966, was made Assistant General Secretary of the Ba'ath party which then staged yet another coup in 1968, this time firmly establishing Bakr as president of the country.

Saddam Hussein was now put in charge of the Office of General Relations, a dainty name for a thuggish department for in reality General Relations stood for Secret Security. In addition, rather like Stalin, Saddam began to gather as many government departments under him as possible and slowly but surely made himself indispensable to the 'father leader' Bakr. Saddam also ensured that all threats to the party, and therefore his position, whether real or imagined, were dealt with swiftly. One man in particular fell victim to this, Colonel Hajj Sirri who was not a Ba'athist and therefore posed a slight threat to an already neurotic Saddam. Sirri was arrested and accused of being a CIA agent, after which he was subjected to endless interrogations and brutal torture. Sirri however, would not give in, so finally his torturers pulled their trump card and threatened to rape all the female members of his family. It was too much to bear and subsequently Sirri told his interrogators exactly what they wanted to hear; shortly afterwards he was sentenced to death and hanged.

This wasn't the first brutal act Saddam Hussein had instigated and certainly it wasn't to be his last. A short time later, thirty men were, on the flimsiest of evidence, accused of spying for Israel. Saddam, who was by this time in charge of all government propaganda, decided to make a huge show of the case and had the accused men's trials televised. The outcome of the trial almost went without saying, each of the accused being found guilty and being sentenced to death. But further to this, after the sentences had been carried out, the corpses were left hanging in Liberation Square for over a day. The public was urged to view the bodies and when president Bakr arrived along with Saddam, they were to enjoy a huge welcome from the crowd who cheered and applauded their appearance.

Buoyed up by these two successes and knowing that the elderly and ailing Bakr trusted him implicitly, Saddam now turned his attention on the Iraqi army. This was the only real threat to the new regime, but rather than antagonize the regular forces, Saddam instead set up a paramilitary organization called the Popular Army which would fall under his direct control. Other 'reforms' included restricting the activities of all known Ba'athist opponents and to this end Saddam had seventeen sons and grandsons of one such man, Sayyed Muhsin Al Hakim, hanged. The longer Saddam was in power, the stronger his stranglehold over the country. As the journalist and author, Säid Aburish notes, 'Saddam's twin approach to the consolidation of Ba'athist power continued until the end of 1973. First, enemies were neutralized, be they individuals, ethnic or religious groups or political parties. Simultaneously, ambitious social and economic programmes were pursued at breakneck speed.'[4]

With reference to the former, in December 1974 Saddam had five Shia clerics executed for posing a threat to the

Ba'athists and over the following few months expelled more than 200,000 Shias over the border into Iran. But none of that compares to what occurred next, when in 1979, Saddam forced General Bakr to resign – an act which was officially put down to Bakr's ill health.

Saddam Hussein now declared himself President of Iraq: he had total control over his country and he was not about to relinquish it, despite outside calls for the overthrow of his government. And from where did these outside calls originate? From Iraq's neighbour, Iran, whose own government had, in 1979, changed to an anti-Ba'athist regime. Suddenly, Ayatollah Khomeini (who had taken over the reins of power from the Shah of Iran) was encouraging the Iraqi Shias to overthrow their Ba'ath leader. It was a recipe that was bound to lead to disaster and sure enough, in September 1980 Iraq, responding to a series of border invasions by Iran, mounted a full-scale offensive (using over 300,000 troops) against its neighbour. Saddam himself ran the campaign from a bunker under his presidential palace, yet despite appearances he wasn't removed from the action, far from it; he controlled every military decision from bombing campaigns to minor skirmishes. In addition, Saddam also kept a close watch on internal affairs, never for a moment releasing his grip over his own government. As the war dragged on, so conditions within Iraq itself deteriorated. A sure sign of Saddam's nervousness during this period was that he increased the number of people employed by the secret security ten-fold and it is said that between 1981-1982 over 3,000 mainly Shia civilians were executed. But perhaps the most notorious of all Saddam's actions during this period (apart from implementing a chemical weapons programme) occurred during a cabinet meeting in March 1982 when Saddam, asking his Minister of Health, Riyadh Ibrahim, to step out of the room with him for a moment, took out a gun and shot him, afterwards returning to the meeting as if nothing had happened.

By 1983, the Iran-Iraq war had reached stalemate. Thousands of lives had been lost on both sides and yet nothing had been achieved and neither country was nearer a resolution.

Then Saddam began using both mustard and nerve gas (in contravention of the 1899 Hague and 1925 Geneva Conventions). One of the worst-hit sites was the Kurdish town of Halabja (population 45,000) in the north of Iraq which had a combination of mustard gas (which affects the skin, eyes and membranes of the nose, throat and lungs) together with nerve agents Sarin, Tabun and VX, dropped on it. It is believed that due to these raids between 3,200–5,000 people were killed, and even those who did manage to survive, suffered long-term health problems. In addition, the use of even more chemical weapons was implemented during what became known as Iraq's *Anfal* (named after the Muslim victory in the battle of Badr which is spoken of in the Koran). Once again, the weapons were directed against the Kurds, whom Saddam feared wanted to create an independent Kurdistan. During this campaign it has been estimated that between 50,000-100,000 Kurdish men, women and children were either killed by chemical weapons, executed, or displaced, while their villages, farms and mosques were razed to the ground.

Finally, in July 1988, after almost nine years of war, Iran was forced to accept defeat and, though a peace treaty wasn't signed, there was an agreement to end hostilities. However, the toll of the war not only on Iran, but more importantly on Iraq, was enormous. Iraq's treasury was practically empty, people's morale was at an all-time low and corruption was rife. Yet despite these setbacks, Saddam believed the best way to strengthen his position in the Middle East and turn his country into the type of force people couldn't ignore, was to continue developing his chemical weapons. To this end he siphoned off as much money as he could from both civil and military projects and despite his people being on the brink of starvation, never once stinted when it came to financially supporting his chemical weapons programme. However, when it came to buying equipment from abroad, Saddam faced increasing frustration the West began denying him credit, on top of which the US started intercepting various shipments of 'unconventional' weapons to Iraq.

Infuriated, Saddam began to act in an increasingly erratic

manner. Similarly, his son Udday Hussein[5] (whom several commentators have described as being mentally deficient) also began behaving in an unpredictable way. In October 1988, Udday gatecrashed a party that was being attended by the wife of the Egyptian President, Hosni Mubarak, shooting dead a man by the name of Hanna Geogo. Initially Saddam, in an attempt to make an example of his son, had him imprisoned and then sent into exile in Switzerland, but less than four months after Geogo was murdered, Udday returned to Iraq and was given a presidential pardon. Not long afterwards, Udday then initiated a fight with his cousin and not only damaged his liver, but also left him in a coma. This time Saddam did nothing to punish his son and no doubt it was because of this lack of patriarchal disapproval that Udday then felt free to gather a band of thugs around him and began trafficking in drugs and arms.

But Saddam was no less outrageous or vicious than his tearaway son, for it was during this period (with his country still on the brink of poverty) that he began to spend vast amounts of money building palaces. One such building, which was started in 1988, took a further eight years to construct. Another had blue marble floors imported from Argentina at a cost of $3,000-4,000 per square metre. In addition to this, Saddam also designed and built an Iraqi equivalent to the French Arc de Triomphe in order to celebrate the end of the *Anfal* programme. But at the back of Saddam's mind was the constant pressure of where to find more money, how to make Iraq's oil fields pay greater dividends.

At this time the small kingdom of Kuwait, whose territory bordered Iraq's own was, to Saddam's way of thinking, exceeding its oil production quotas as set by OPEC and therefore lowering the price Iraq could charge for its own resources. Saddam also accused the Kuwaiti government of stealing oil from the Rumailah fields and establishing both military and civilian installations and bases on Iraqi territory. Angered by these so-called outrages, Saddam began threatening to invade Kuwait and, despite a meeting in Jeddah held on 31 July 1990 between Saudi, Kuwaiti and Iraqi officials who had come together with the sole intention of averting war, Saddam would not be pacified. In the early hours of 2 August 1990, the Iraqi army marched on its neighbour and within less than half a day had occupied Kuwait whose Emir, Sheik Jaber al-Ahmed al-Sabah fled into exile in Saudi Arabia. What followed were seven nightmarish months for the Kuwaitis whose lives were turned upside down as Iraqi troops indulged in an orgy of looting, pillaging, and torture. During the first days of the invasion, Amnesty International in London received several reports that hundreds of Kuwaiti military personnel had been taken off to detention and torture centres. Essentially, what was happening in Kuwait was an extension of the type of terror wielded by the Ba'athist regime within Iraq itself. The same instruments of torture were used and, as the following extract demonstrates, the same methods.

'The human rights organization [Amnesty International] has interviewed scores of people who have fled Kuwait,' reported one observer, 'and two of its representatives have just returned from Bahrain, where they talked with victims and eyewitnesses of abuses. "Their testimony builds up a horrifying picture of widespread arrests, torture under interrogation, summary executions and mass extra-judicial killings," Amnesty International said… Some people have also been arrested or killed for failing to replace photos of the Emir with those of Iraq's President Saddam Hussein…Some have been given electric shocks or suffered prolonged beatings to sensitive parts of their bodies. Others have had their limbs broken, their hair plucked out with pincers, their finger and toe nails pulled out, and were threatened with sexual assault or execution. "We cannot even publish more details on former torture victims, in case they or their families are identified and suffer further reprisals," Amnesty International said.'[6]

In addition to the human rights abuses, government buildings, along with hotels, nightclubs, hospitals and schools were ransacked and foreign nationals had to go into hiding for fear they would be used as part of Saddam's 'human shield' against the threat of retaliation by the West.

And retaliate the West did. Initially the UN Security

Council passed a resolution (660) condemning the invasion and demanding an immediate withdrawal by Iraq, otherwise sanctions would be implemented. When this failed to move Saddam, British Prime Minister, Margaret Thatcher began urging US President George Bush to stand up to Saddam and threaten him with war. Not long afterwards, on 7 August, US Defence Secretary, Richard Cheney met with King Fahd of Saudi Arabia and requested permission to station US troops on Saudi soil as a precaution against an invasion by Iraq. But this threat, far from persuading Saddam to move out of Kuwait, prompted him instead to declare Kuwait the nineteenth province of Iraq for historically, since the time of the Ottoman Empire, Iraq had always considered Kuwait to be part and parcel of its territory.

Naturally, the UN was infuriated and promptly issued another resolution condemning Saddam; only this time the USSR also joined in the condemnation, something which came as a huge blow to the Iraqi leader. Suddenly, he was out in the cold, without a friendly face in sight, but due to a combination of stubbornness and arrogance, things were about to become even worse.

On 1 September 1990, Margaret Thatcher announced that Saddam Hussein would be charged with war crimes against humanity, while on 9 September President Bush met with Mikhail Gorbachov, the two men jointly agreeing to present a united front against Iraq in accordance with the UN. Subsequently, an international coalition was formed after which thousands upon thousands of troops from all over the world gathered within the region. With General Norman Schwarzkopf at the helm, a battle plan was quickly assembled.

By November all diplomatic approaches to end the crisis had come to an end and the UN, tired of Saddam's dissembling, set a deadline for his country's withdrawal from Kuwait (SCR 678, 29 November 1990), adding that a failure to do so would guarantee the use of 'all necessary means' to oust Iraq from the region. Shortly afterwards, on the morning of 16 January 1991, massive air strikes began against Iraq and the words 'Desert Storm' entered the English language.

To begin with the strikes were against military targets in both Iraq and Kuwait, as well as singling out bridges, power stationers, oil refineries, airports, etc. As was his way, in order to avoid being targeted, Saddam moved from one presidential palace to another, sleeping in bunkers specially built in case of war. It was the best he could do in a bad situation as the Iraqi air force was no match for that of the allies who, night after night, bombarded the country. It was difficult to imagine how Saddam felt he could ever achieve victory and yet, on 26 January, Iraqi soldiers, on the direct instructions of their president, briefly invaded Saudi Arabia and occupied the town of Kafji, only to be ousted two days later. In general, the Iraqi troops were tired and hungry. Some troops claimed they had gone without food for several days and because some of the bombing had taken out hospitals, medical provisions were also in short supply. President Bush did not let up the pressure on Saddam, demanding that he withdraw his troops from Kuwait by 23 February or else face a ground war. In retaliation, Saddam set the Kuwaiti oilfields alight and this in turn began an oil spill of biblical proportions. Suddenly the air overhead was filled with mile-wide clouds of acrid black smoke.

Unsurprisingly, this was the last act of a desperate man for shortly afterwards, on 3 March 1991, General Schwarzkopf and Saudi General Khalid Bin Sultan met and accepted the surrender of Iraqi Generals Sultan Hashim Ahmad and Salah Abid Mohammed. By this time US and allied forces had already forayed deep into Iraq itself, but they had stopped short of occupying Baghdad and taking out their ultimate target, Saddam Hussein. It was a decision that, over a decade later, would come back to haunt them. But at the time, instead of finishing the job they had come to do, President Bush together with General Schwarzkopf began inciting the Iraqi people to rise up and remove Saddam from power themselves.

Believing that the US would aid them in this plan, on 5 March 1991 the Shias in southern Iraq did rise up in open rebellion. Suddenly armed insurrection broke out in Basra and Nassiriya with thousands of Iraqis shouting for Saddam's demise and by the time the unrest reached the Shia cities of

Najjaf and Karbala, it was all-out civil war. Nor were the Shias alone in their fight, for shortly after the insurrection began, Iraqi Kurds in the north of the country joined in the rebellion. They were calling on the US to stand behind what they had begun and come to their aid, but President Bush refused. Some people say this was because it was a Shia uprising and if the US helped, then it would be tantamount to approving Shia-controlled Iran, or worse still, that Iraq would later become an Islamic fundamentalist state. Whatever the reason, the allies remained stationary; this was going to be a fight between the rebels and Saddam alone.

Initially Saddam appointed his cousin, (best known by the soubriquet Chemical Ali) to crush by any means necessary the rebellion in the south while in Baghdad Saddam gave his troops shoot-to-kill orders in case anyone in the capital dared take up arms. Unfortunately for the rebels, who might have expected support from their Shia neighbour Iran, none was forthcoming. The Iranians, all too aware that any show of involvement would only infuriate the Americans, simply sat back and watched.

Chemical Ali swiftly reoccupied Basra while other divisions under his command conquered Karbala and Najjaf. It was a bloodbath, with between 50,000–200,000 killed, hospitals blown to pieces and hundreds of men, women and children tortured. One report told of an entire family being taken up in a helicopter and thrown out alive to their deaths. Other reports described how anyone thought to be a rebel sympathizer had their ears cut off. And that was only in southern Iraq. The Kurds in the north also came under attack and, with no sign that the allies would lift a finger to help, Iraqi troops let loose their most base instincts, beginning a killing spree which ended with over 100,000 Kurds dead or wounded and in the region of 2 million either missing or displaced. These were statistics that the world couldn't ignore and thankfully (albeit too late for many) it didn't.

On 10 April 1991 Operation Provide Comfort was instigated by the allied forces to protect the Kurds and, by creating a no-fly zone in the north, giving them a place of safety in which to live. Despite this setback to his plans, Saddam Hussein emerged from the whole sorry tale as the supreme leader of his country and, if it can be believed, he was in an even stronger position politically than when the war had first begun.

The UN now imposed sanctions on Iraq (sanctions which were most strictly upheld by the US and Britain) after which there also began a long campaign to locate Saddam's weapons of mass destruction. As is well-documented, this campaign became a lengthy (stretching over twelve years) game of cat and mouse with Saddam at first agreeing to UN inspectors then objecting to them, after which he would recant and agree. But tragically, if it was no more than a game to him, for the Iraqi people it proved far more devastating for at the same time as the outside world was imposing strict measures (including food and medical embargoes) against Iraq, so they were also suffering under Saddam's day-to-day oppression. For them it was a no-win situation; the more his people suffered, the more Saddam could turn round to the world at large and say that for humanity's sake, the sanctions ought to be lifted. But nothing was about to happen unless the UN inspectors were allowed to go about their business so the result was, for twelve years, stalemate. In the interim, Saddam's crimes against his own people continued, most notably in the case of the Marsh Arabs whose land Saddam drained by diverting water, which should have run into the marshes, into a third river (alongside the Euphrates and Tigris). When the Marsh Arabs rebelled at what they saw as a direct threat to their way of life, Saddam ordered his Republican Guard to go in and quash the uprising. This they did, killing thousands in their wake and displacing tens of thousands more. Saddam continued to wreak havoc, not only on the civilian population, but also on members of his own government and extended family. Even though the majority of his government were from his own region of Tikrit, he had many of them executed for fear they were plotting against him. As far as his family was concerned, in 1996 the husbands of two of his daughters defected to Saudi Arabia in fear of their lives, only to be wooed back to Iraq by Saddam and consequently executed.

And so the killing continued, until that is 11 September 2001 which, as in the case of Osama bin Laden and the Taliban, proved a watershed date.

Immediately after 11 September the US directed the full force of its wrath against those it saw as the main perpetrators i.e. the *al-Qaeda* network and Osama bin Laden. However, shortly after the war in Afghanistan, attention focused on Saddam Hussein. In his State of the Union speech George W. Bush declared a 'War on Terror' targeting Iraq, along with Iran, North Korea and Syria, as major players in the 'Axis of Evil'. America was determined to show who was boss and although Prime Minister Tony Blair persuaded Bush to take the UN route, on 20 March 2003, the war finally began.

By 3 April US troops had reached Saddam International airport, a mere ten miles outside Baghdad city centre and by 8 April they were operating from inside Baghdad itself. Yet despite a concerted effort to track down and kill Saddam, (just like that other enemy of the US Osama bin Laden) he evaded capture. What couldn't be denied the allied forces however, was the uncovering of a mass grave in which it was believed lay the corpses of up to 15,000 people, missing since the Shiite uprising in 1991. Tragically similar mass graves were found throughout the country.

'Each cut of the workers' spades unearths another collection of reddened bones and soiled clothing,' wrote Ed Vulliamy for the *Observer* on 25 May 2003. 'Some of the dead were wearing military fatigues, others were clad in sports or everyday clothes when they were killed, a track suit here, a pin-striped-suit there…This is what happened to the victims of Musayyib: in the wake of the insurrection, anyone suspected with taking part was ordered or taken to an outdoor space, and boarded onto trucks and buses. The vehicles were then driven from the river valley out into nowhere. There, the captives were lined up – hands tied and blindfolded – and pushed into the bottom of the pits. And in the earthy tomb, they were machine-gunned and the dirt replaced by bulldozer, by way of crude cover.'

Despite these and other gruesome discoveries, including torture chambers and Secret Security files bulging with photographs of dead Iraqis, some with their necks and faces slashed, others with their eyes gouged out and their genitals blackened, still no one could locate either the Iraqi president, nor his weapons of mass destruction. The former, it was thought might have slipped over the border into Syria, but as for the latter it is (on going to press) still a matter of some embarrassment for the coalition forces that nothing has, to date, come to light.

And what next for Iraq? For the foreseeable future it appears that America together with Britain is to occupy the country with a view to establishing some kind of stability. Whether this is possible given the Iraqi peoples' (some might argue, justifiable) distrust of the West is yet to be seen, but on recent evidence the outlook is bleak for on 24 June 2003 six British Royal Military Police were slaughtered and a further eight soldiers injured in two attacks in the southeastern town of Majar al-Kabir. Doubtless, if Saddam Hussein is still alive, reports of this incident, along with all the other recent tragedies, will put a smile on the dictator's face. After all, when he was in power Saddam enjoyed nothing better than raining down pain and torment on all those who surrounded him.

OSAMA BIN LADEN

THE DAY OF THE JACKAL

*We don't consider it a crime if we tried to have nuclear,
chemical, biological weapons. If I have indeed acquired these
weapons, then I thank God for enabling me to do so.*

OSAMA BIN LADEN[1]

On 26 February 1993 a yellow Ford Econoline van came to a
halt in the underground parking area of the World Trade
Center complex in Manhattan, New York. Seconds later two
men alighted from the vehicle and jumped into a red car that
had been following them, but not before one of the two set light
to four, 20-foot-long fuses which were attached to a massive
bomb that sat in the back of the van. Twelve minutes later the
inevitable happened, the bomb exploded, tearing through
offices, stairwells and reinforced concrete floors. By the end of
the day six people were known to have died in addition to
which 1,042 injuries were sustained. It was a terrible day for
America; one that it was hard to believe had occurred, but
miraculously the twin towers had withstood the blast. It could
have been so much worse. What if the bomb, which had been
positioned next to a wall which housed one quarter of the
support columns for Tower One, had done its work and
brought Tower One crashing down into Tower Two? The image
was unimaginable. After all, the World Trade Center Complex
was more like a city within a city, comprising as it did seven
massive buildings as well as a labyrinthine underworld of
shops, garages, restaurants and offices. In addition to this, the
two towers also symbolized America's commercial success.
Never mind the loss of life that would have occurred had the
bomb been more effective; the blow to America's self-esteem
would have been devastating.

Jump ahead eight years. It is now the morning of 11
September 2001 and at Boston Airport, United Airlines Flight

175 is departing for Los Angeles. The aeroplane is carrying 56 passengers, two pilots and seven flight attendants, but just after takeoff the plane is hijacked and diverted to New York. Less than one minute later, a second Boeing aircraft, American Airlines Flight 11 also departs from Boston to fly to Los Angeles and is also hijacked just after takeoff. This time there are 81 passengers on board, two pilots and nine flight attendants. Similarly, at Newark Airport in New Jersey, United Airlines 93, which is bound for San Francisco is hijacked and at Washington Dulles International Airport, American Airlines Flight 77 bound for Los Angeles is hijacked. With each of the four aircraft now on a course of destruction, it is only a matter of time before disaster strikes and two of America's most important cities are reduced to war-like zones of fear and carnage.

8.46a.m. and American Airlines Flight 11 crashes into the North Tower of the World Trade Center. Unsurprisingly, the devastation is horrific. Huge clouds of smoke billow out from where the plane has driven a hole in the side of the building. There are flames, twisted metal and worst of all, some of the people who are trapped in the building begin jumping from its windows to certain death.

Minutes later, to the horror of those watching from the street below, a second passenger jet crashes into the South Tower somewhere around the sixtieth storey. But the carnage does not stop there. In Washington DC another of the hijacked aircraft crashes into the south-west face of the Pentagon while in Pennsylvania, United Flight 93 plunges into a wooded area, after the passengers confront their hijackers.

Destabilized by the impact of Flight 175, at a few minutes after 10.00a.m. the South Tower of the World Trade Center collapses, quickly followed by that of the North Tower. Not since Pearl Harbor has the United States experienced such an onslaught of attacks and when President Bush makes his first statement to the nation he vows to 'find those responsible and bring them to justice'. Two days later Secretary of State, Colin Powell identifies one man behind 11 September; his name is Osama bin Laden.

It is safe to say that before 11 September 2001, despite being

America's most wanted terrorist suspect, to the average man in the street, the name of Osama bin Laden (sometimes spelt Usama Bin Laden) meant very little. Born in Riyadh, Saudi Arabia in 1957, Osama bin Laden is the seventeenth son (he has between 50-53 half brothers and sisters) of one of the Middle East's most successful businessmen, Mohammad bin Oud bin Laden, and his eleventh wife, who is of Syrian origin.

Osama's father hailed originally from the southern Yemeni province of Hadramaout, but eventually ended up in Jeddah after Saudi Arabia was established as a kingdom in its own right in 1932. There is some confusion about bin Laden Snr's employment during these early years, but most sources have it that he worked as a porter in Jeddah port, before building up a small construction company. Subsequently, he set about winning several much-sought-after contracts from the Saudi royal family to build, amongst other things, the royal palace at Jeddah. The project was a huge success, not only financially, but also with respect to his relationship with King Saud and other members of the royal family, including Crown Prince Faisal. Building contracts soon flowed in his direction and bin Laden Snr quickly become a very rich man. In the early 1960s, Faisal came to the throne helped, it is said, by Mohammed bin Laden who offered to pay the wages of the Saudi civil service for a period of several months due to there being an enormous financial glitch in the treasury's coffers after King Saud's departure. The offer paid huge dividends, for thereafter King Faisal decreed that all construction work in the kingdom was to be given to the bin Laden family group, on top of which Mohammad was given a position in the government, that of Minister for Public Works.

With so many lucrative contracts under his belt it is no surprise that Mohammad bin Laden's company should be so successful. In fact, it is not only responsible for constructing many of the most eminent buildings in Saudi Arabia, but also for re-building much of Kuwait and Beirut (after their respective wars), and according to several financial reports, the company was estimated (*circa* the mid-nineties) to have a turnover of over $35 billion.

Despite his great wealth, Mohammad bin Laden is said to have been a modest man who was, first and foremost, a devoted Muslim. As such, he brought up all of his children in the Wahhabite tradition (a branch of Islam that originated in Saudi Arabia during the eighteenth century), teaching them to respect and obey the laws of Islam. Nonetheless, although greatly affected by his father's influence, Osama bin Laden did not always respect his Islamic upbringing. Certainly in his late teens, when he spent a certain amount of time in Beirut, he enjoyed all the pleasures that a western-influenced city had to offer. At that time the Lebanese capital was full of nightclubs, bars and prostitutes and between 1973 and 1975 (i.e. before civil war tore Lebanon in two) the young Osama appeared to forget his strict upbringing and pleasured himself to the full. But the high-life was a short-lived affair, for not long after 1975, Osama appears to have experienced a change of heart and instead of continuing to enjoy the trappings of the dissolute West, he set himself on a far more rigid course of action. Firstly, he married a young Syrian girl after which he enrolled in a management and civil engineering course not, as many of his brothers had done in London or New York, but at the King Abdul Aziz University in Jeddah where he could follow the teachings of Islam with less distractions.

Two crucial events subsequently occurred which must have influenced the young student who was already leaning towards a fundamentalist approach to life. A handful of Muslim scholars began to preach that the war in Lebanon, and in particular the destruction of Beirut, was God's way of punishing the city for its adoption of Western values. Then, King Faisal was assassinated by his nephew, who was known to be mentally unstable, and again the scholars pronounced that it was a judgement on the young man who had been in America and had therefore been exposed to a dissolute lifestyle. That such claims were taken seriously might seem risible to most western readers, but to an impressionable young man, brought up in the Muslim tradition and searching for a meaning to his life, the doctrine these scholars preached and all that their claims suggested, made a great deal of sense. Still,

Osama had not entirely broken with his family, or the influence that it wielded. He was intrigued by the business side of the empire and as such attended many meetings alongside his father and brothers. But it must have been difficult to make his mark in a family with fifty or so children sparring for attention and several biographers have suggested that one sibling in particular, Salim bin Laden, who was to be Mohammad's successor, caused Osama to feel most jealous.

In the early 1970s, Mohammad bin Laden died in a plane crash and with his death came a great deal of internal warring within the bin Laden household as brothers and uncles all vied for positions of power. As is the Saudi style, most of the disputes were settled by bestowing vast amounts of money on each claimant and to this end it is thought that Osama was bequeathed in the region of £300 million.

Osama was now in a strong position to move forward with his life, begin a career and start a family. He had an education and money behind him, but he was a rebel without a cause until, in 1979, one suddenly presented itself to him.

On 26 December 1979, Leonid Brezhnev sent Soviet troops into Afghanistan. Millions of Muslims all over the world, including bin Laden, were incandescent with rage. It was the perfect excuse for which to take up arms, but bin Laden, not one to dirty his hands with the nuts and bolts of war, decided instead to use his vast wealth as a means of training and supplying Muslim soldiers to protect Afghanistan from the invaders.

To this end bin Laden travelled to Pakistan where he met up with a notorious Palestinian fundamentalist, Abdallah Azzam who promised that he could put bin Laden in touch with several disparate groups of Islamic fighters, men who were committed to the cause but lacked the finances to put their plans into action.

Soon afterwards, bin Laden returned to Saudi Arabia where he began touting for support amongst the highest echelons of the Saudi government. Nor was he disappointed, for several key government ministers promised to help out financially and shortly afterwards bin Laden returned to Pakistan where he and Azzam put together what would later become known as *al-Qaeda*, which is an Arabic word meaning, 'The Base'.

These bases or camps would, with bin Laden's money, fly young men into Afghanistan, train them as soldiers, kit them out with as much weaponry as was required and, should the worst happen, even pay their families compensation should any of them die. Bin Laden also formed an organization called the Islamic Salvation Foundation which was set up solely to manage the vast sums of money being donated to the cause. Together with Azzam, he established another organization called the Maktab al-Khidimat (MAK) also known as the Office of Services of the Mujaheddin whose main aim was to recruit more and more young men from around the world to fight the good fight. Egyptians, Lebanese, Turks, Saudi Arabians all joined the cause.

Bin Laden was in his element. Not only was he raising vast amounts of cash by endearing himself to kings, princes and businessmen alike, he was also actively involved in transporting equipment such as bulldozers into Afghanistan in order to rebuild roads and dig trenches. And although he was best known as a 'back-room boy', i.e. someone who didn't actively participate in the fighting, there were times when he did, in particular during early 1986 when, along with some 100 other men, he defended the Afghan village of Jadji from Soviet attack. It was to be a life-forming experience, for not only did the Afghan Arab soldiers manage to keep the Soviets at bay for over one month, they also killed over a dozen of the enemy. Eventually, the Soviets retreated, leaving bin Laden to conclude that not only was the Soviet army beatable, but that he himself was invincible. There are countless tales told which back up this theory, tales of Osama surviving Scud missile attacks and stories where he vanquished opponents left, right and centre. But there have also been reports that, far from being a much-admired leader of men, Osama was often regarded as a petulant, if somewhat dangerous, child. Take for example this account by the BBC World Affairs Editor, John Simpson:

'I was filming a group of mujaheddin in Afghanistan as they fired mortars at the nearby town of Jalalabad. An impressive-looking Arab in beard and white robes [bin Laden], one of the many fundamentalist volunteers fighting alongside the mujaheddin, suddenly appeared. Jumping up on a wall, he screamed that we were infidels and that the mujaheddin should kill us at once. They grinned and shrugged their shoulders, so he ran over to a truck driver and offered him $500 (£312) to run us down. The truck driver grinned, too. Then the tall Arab ran off to the mujaheddin's sleeping quarters and threw himself on to one of the beds, beating his fists on the pillow in frustration. My colleagues and I stood and watched him with a mixture of embarrassment and relief.'[2]

Despite this comic portrayal, bin Laden was nonetheless a formidable opponent; a man with huge sums of money at his disposal as well as an uncanny knack for making friends in high places. During the Afghan war he forged several friendships, one of which was with Ayman al-Zawahiri, who was to become the head of Islamic Jihad. More surprisingly, however, were the alliances made between bin Laden and the American government which was also trying to evict Russia from Afghan soil. In fact, over the course of three years, America together with Saudi Arabia poured over £300 million into support for the mujaheddin. But the allegiance was a short-lived affair and after the Soviets finally withdrew in defeat from Afghanistan, the Arab Afghans immediately turned their venom on the US and its allies in the Middle East.

Now in his early thirties, Osama bin Laden returned to Saudi Arabia. Initially he was hailed as a hero, a man of principals who had poured money into a worthy cause and who had overthrown the second greatest power in the world. But after years of leading a frugal life in the less than hospitable Afghani landscape, Saudi Arabia came as a terrible shock. Everywhere bin Laden went he saw evidence of Western influence, people disobeying Islamic law, tourists openly drinking alcohol, women flaunting themselves on the street. Suddenly bin Laden was on the warpath again to which end he swiftly re-established his *al-Qaeda* network, (which towards the latter part of the 1990s the CIA and FBI identified as being responsible for several terrorist attacks on America's interests, including the 1993 World Trade Center bombing, the 1996 killing of 19 US soldiers in Saudi Arabia, and the 1998 US embassy bombings in Kenya and Tanzania).

But it was yet another world-shattering event that was to further compound Osama bin Laden's hatred of the West. In August 1990 the Iraqi President, Saddam Hussein, ordered his troops into the kingdom of Kuwait, at which point the Saudi government invited thousands of American, British and other allied troops onto their soil, ostensibly to protect it from invasion. Whatever the reason, it was all too much for bin Laden who now turned his wrath on his fellow countrymen, condemning them for aligning themselves with infidels. Shortly afterwards, he fled Saudi, having been confined to Jeddah for his staunch opposition to the US presence in his country[3] travelling first back to Afghanistan and then to Sudan.

At this point Osama was in his mid-thirties. He had three wives and, following in his late father's footsteps, he had sired fifteen children. However, it was not his family that occupied his time while in the Sudan, for instead he turned his attention to establishing further *al-Qaeda* camps and purchasing as many weapons as he could, including Semtex, from as disparate countries as China and Czechoslovakia.

By 1991, US and allied troops had succeeded in winning the Gulf War but, rather than returning home, the US established a large military presence in Saudi Arabia uncomfortably close to two of the most holy shrines in Islam, Mecca and Medina. Osama bin Laden was once again filled with rage and it is said that from this point on he allied himself and his organization with Shiite Muslim terrorist groups such as Hezbollah. In addition, he also vowed to attack any US troops stationed in either Saudi Arabia or Yemen as well as those stationed in the Horn of Africa.

True to his word, shortly afterwards on 29 December 1992 a bomb exploded in a hotel in Aden, Yemen, killing two Austrian tourists. The intended targets, US troops, had already left the hotel on their way to a humanitarian mission, Operation Restore Hope, in Somalia.

In quick succession, two more terrorist attacks occurred. On

26 February 1993 the World Trade Center was bombed and on 3 and 4 October of the same year 18 US soldiers were killed in an urban attack in Mogadishu, Somalia. (This event was later turned into a major feature film, *Black Hawk Down* directed by Ridley Scott, 2001).

US intelligence networks were in no doubt that *al-Qaeda* was behind both attacks and in 1995,when Ramzi Yousef, the man accused of the World Trade Center bombing, was captured, several documents came to light linking him financially with Osama bin Laden and also pointing to the fact that he had stayed at a guest house financed by bin Laden in Pakistan.

Far from denying his involvement in these barbarous acts, bin Laden revelled in his notoriety.

'It is true,' he said, 'that my companions fought with Farah Adid's forces against the US troops in Somalia. But we were fighting against US terrorism. Under the cover of [the] United Nations, the United States tried to establish its bases in Somalia so that it could get control over Sudan and Yemen. My associates killed the Americans in collaboration with Farah Adid. We are not ashamed of our Jihad. In one explosion 100 Americans were killed, then 18 more were killed in fighting. One day our men shot down an American helicopter. The pilot got out. We caught him, tied his legs and dragged him through the streets. After that 28,000 US soldiers fled Somalia. The Americans are cowards.'[4] Of course, bin Laden had exaggerated the casualty figures in his favour, but the main issue was clear, he would attack US troops at every opportunity and in the process suffer not one iota of guilt.

In 1993, after the World Trade Center attack, the FBI and CIA identified Osama bin Laden as a serious threat to US security. Tracing back links with Ramzi Yousef and his co-conspirators was a complicated affair, but it soon dawned on the investigators that what they had on their hands was a major 'blowback' situation from the time when the US had supported the militant Afghan groups during the Soviet invasion of that country. 'We did spawn a monster in Afghanistan,' said Richard Murphy, Assistant Secretary of State for Near East and

South Asian Relations during the Reagan era. 'Once the Soviets were gone [the Afghan Arabs] were looking around for other targets, and Mr Osama bin Laden has settled on the United States as the source of all evil.'[5]

Suddenly bin Laden's name was on everybody's lips. There was no doubting his involvement in the World Trade Center bombing and now he was also linked to the events in Mogadishu. But bin Laden wasn't about to rest on his laurels, quite the contrary. On 13 November 1995 five American servicemen together with two Indians were killed by a truck bombing outside a US-operated Saudi National Guard training centre in Riyadh. Disingenuously, bin Laden denied any involvement in the attack, but praised its outcome. Subsequently, four Saudi men were arrested and beheaded in Riyadh's main square before the American investigators could interview them. This in turn lead the Americans to the conclusion that the executions were carried out so swiftly in order to prevent them realising the full extent of bin Laden's association with the terrorists. Whatever the reason, the four men all admitted being firm supporters of bin Laden and his fight against Western infidels.

By this time the Sudanese government was coming under increasing international pressure to expel bin Laden and finally, in May 1996, he moved back to Afghanistan where a large number of former Islamic fundamentalists had formed themselves into a militia best known to the West as the Taliban. The Taliban introduced strict Sharia Law and forced the entire country to follow suit which meant amongst other things that all men were to attend mosque five times a day, that women weren't allowed to work and had to wear the burqua on pain of death and that all music was banned. It was a harsh, unforgiving regime; nonetheless bin Laden together with his family and several staunch supporters made their way there gladly.

Perhaps this was America's biggest mistake. After all, if it hadn't pressurized the Sudanese government into squeezing bin Laden out of their country into exile in one of the world's most inaccessible territories, then they could have kept a closer eye on their number one terrorist. As it was, bin Laden disappeared off the face of the map, leastways as far as the CIA and FBI were concerned.

But *al-Qaeda* was not so quiet, nor so invisible. On the night of 25 June 1996 a large truck bomb (in excess of 5,000lb) exploded outside a US military residence in Dharran called Khobar Towers. In total nineteen servicemen were killed and countless others were injured. No one knows if bin Laden was behind this attack (some sources believe it was the work of a Saudi Shiite group) although US investigators are convinced bin Laden was responsible.

Shortly after this last terrorist attack a secret, grand jury investigation into bin Laden swung into action in New York. At its head was the FBI together with a woman called Mary Jo White who was the then US Attorney for the Southern District of New York. Their remit was to explore as far as was possible bin Laden's involvement in international terrorism. As if aware of what the US was up to, bin Laden issued a Declaration of Jihad outlining *al-Qaeda's* main goals, i.e. to banish US forces from the Arabian Peninsula, as well as to overthrow the Saudi government, liberate Muslim holy sites and in general support Islamic revolutionary groups all over the globe.

But as well as raising the profile of *al-Qaeda* by issuing this and other such inflammatory statements, bin Laden was also working hard behind the scenes securing friendships and political support from the leaders of his newly adopted country. In particular, he began to cultivate relations with Mullah Mohamed Omar, the supreme leader of the Taliban, buying him houses and showering him with expensive gifts. At the same time, conscious of his own safety and how risky it was to remain in one place too long, bin Laden began what later became a way of life; he never stayed in one place longer than two nights, often camping out in Afghanistan's vast mountain regions or in caves and shacks. The only concession he made to modern-day comforts was to carry a laptop computer and a satellite phone – other than that he took only Islamic books.

By this time America, infuriated by bin Laden's repeated threats against itself and its citizens, decided to track down bin Laden and either assassinate him or, better still, capture him alive. In June 1997 three diplomats, together with a handful of CIA agents, flew to Peshawar to hold secret meetings with members of the Taliban. They made it clear that they would pay a handsome sum of money for information as to their prey's whereabouts. However, the Taliban would not surrender their 'guest' and gave the Americans little or no information. To add insult to injury, in early 1998 bin Laden then issued yet another of his now infamous statements. Together with the Islamic Group, Al Jihad, bin Laden stated that they had formed a coalition called the International Islamic Front for Jihad Against the Jews and Crusaders.

'First, for over seven years the United States has been occupying the lands of Islam in the holiest of places, the Arabian Peninsula, plundering its riches, dictating to its rulers, humiliating its people, terrorizing its neighbours, and turning its bases in the Peninsula into a spearhead through which to fight the neighbouring Muslim peoples... Second, despite the great devastation inflicted on the Iraqi people by the crusader-Zionist alliance...the Americans are once again trying to repeat the horrific massacres...Third, if the Americans' aims behind these wars are religious and economic, the aim is also to serve the Jews' petty state and divert attention from its occupation of Jerusalem and murder of Muslims there.'[6]

If anyone was in any doubt whether bin Laden was serious, they didn't have to wait long to find out, for later that year, on 7 August, two simultaneous bombs exploded at US embassies in Kenya and in Tanzania. The bomb in Nairobi, Kenya, killed 213 people including 12 US nationals and injured more than 4,500 others. The bomb in Dar es Salaam, Tanzania, killed 11 people and injured 85. No Americans died in this second attack, but if ever a gauntlet had been laid down, then this was it.

Shortly afterwards, having been presented with a mass of information on *al-Qaeda* and its links to both embassy bombings, President Clinton ordered a series of Tomahawk cruise missile strikes against bin Laden's training camps in Afghanistan as well as a pharmaceutical plant in Sudan where the Clinton administration were convinced chemical weapons were being produced for bin Laden's sole use. However, if the Americans were hoping to take out bin Laden with their air strikes, they were to be disappointed for not long after the camps had been decimated, American intelligence picked up a radio message from bin Laden praising Allah that he was still alive.

Throughout the Muslim world, Osama bin Laden was now a household name, someone to be admired, praised, followed; a man who had stood up to the arrogant West, a man who would not be ground into submission. Now America was on full alert and every possible way to halt bin Laden's growing network of terror was put into action. The Americans went after bin Laden not only on the ground using undercover operatives; they also tried to block him financially. But still the most wanted terrorist in the world evaded capture. The more the Americans hunted him, the less visible he became, until that is, 11 September 2001.

In the aftermath of the World Trade Center disaster the US was in no doubt who lay behind the attack but it wasn't going to be enough to go after bin Laden alone; the US also wanted to oust the regime that was sheltering him... the Taliban.

'Today,' said President George W Bush, 'our fellow citizens, our way of life, our very freedom came under attack in a series of deliberate and deadly terrorist acts. The victims were in airplanes or in their offices – secretaries, businessmen and women, military and federal workers. Moms and dads. Friends and neighbors...The search is underway for those who are behind these evil acts. I've directed the full resources of our intelligence and law enforcement communities to find those responsible and bring them to justice. We will make no distinction between the terrorists who committed these acts and those who harbor them.'[7]

However, despite repeated calls for the Taliban to surrender bin Laden or face all-out war, the Afghani regime refused to hand over the man whom they regarded as their friend. There was no evidence against bin Laden they said, words which only served to implicate them even deeper with the terrorists. Less than a month after 11 September, the US, together with other western allies, was ready to launch an attack on Afghanistan.

'In what amounted to a final warning to the Islamic fundamentalist regime,' read an article in the *Observer*, 'which is accused of protecting Osama bin Laden and his al-Qaeda terrorist network, Bush said, "Full warning has been given. For those nations that stand with the terrorists, there will be a heavy price."'[8]

Shortly afterwards huge air strikes were launched in an international campaign not only to flush out *al-Qaeda*, but also to punish the regime that had for so long protected bin Laden. Afghanistan was well and truly bombarded and yet, despite the fall of the Taliban, despite bombing raids the like of which the world had never before witnessed, despite repeated attempts to corner their man – Osama bin Laden evaded capture.

It is safe to say that America has never felt more cheated or desperate. Without bin Laden they couldn't claim success and without that success they couldn't be certain when and where bin Laden and his terrorist network would strike again.

Move forward to 12 May 2003. A handful of gunmen and suicide bombers attacked three housing compounds populated mostly by Westerners and other foreign nationals in Riyadh, Saudi Arabia. Nine attackers and twenty-five victims were killed, but despite arresting one of the alleged masterminds behind the bombings, Ali Abd al-Rahman al-Faqasi al-Ghamdi, it almost goes without saying that the most infamous terrorist of them all is still very much, and to America's enormous chagrin, at large.

BIBLIOGRAPHY

ATTILA THE HUN
Howarth, Patrick, *Attila King of the Huns – The Man and The Myth*,
   Robinson, London, 2001
Nicolle, David, *Attila The Hun*, Osprey, Oxford, 2000

TORQUEMADA
Baigent, Michael and Leigh, Richard, *The Inquisition*, Penguin,
   London, 2000
Edwards, John, *The Spanish Inquisition*, Tempus, Stroud, 1999
Kamen, Henry, *Inquisition and Society in Spain in the 16th and 17th
Centuries*, Weidenfeld & Nicolson, London, 1985
Peters, Edward, *Inquisition*, University of California Press, 1988
Roth, C., *The Spanish Inquisition*, R. Hale, London, 1937

VLAD THE IMPALER
McNally, Raymond T. and Florescu, Radu, *Dracula: Prince of Many Faces:
His Life and Times*, Little, Boston, 1989
Treptow, Kurt W., *Vlad III Dracula*, Oxford, 2000

FRANCISCO PIZARRO
Bernard, Carmen, *The Incas – Empire of Blood and Gold*,
   Thames & Hudson, 1996
Innes, Hammond, *The Conquistadors*, Collins, London, 1969
Kirkpatrick F. A., *The Spanish Conquistadors*, Black, London, 1946
Wachtel, Nathan, *The Vision of the Vanquished – the Spanish Conquest
of Peru through Indian Eyes*, Harvester Press, 1977

IVAN IV

Graham, Stephen, *Ivan the Terrible: Life of Ivan IV of Russia*, Archon, Connecticut, 1968

Hosking, Geoffrey, *Russia and The Russians: A History from Rus to the Russian Federation*, Belknap, Harvard University Press, 2001

Troyat, Henri, *Ivan the Terrible*, Phoenix Press, London, 1984

RASPUTIN

Lincoln, W. B., *The Romanovs*, Weidenfeld & Nicolson, London, 1981

Moynahan, Brian, *Rasputin – The Saint Who Sinned*, Arum, London, 1997

Radzinsky, Edvard, *From Wastrel Monk to Political Power – Rasputin: The Last Word*, Weidenfeld & Nicolson, London, 2000

Xenofontova, Lyudmila (trans.), *The Romanovs – Love, Power and Tragedy*, Leppi, Italy, 1993

JOSEF STALIN

Conquest, Robert, *The Great Terror – A Reassessment*, Pimlico Books, London, 1990

Conquest, Robert, *Stalin – Breaker of Nations*, Phoenix, London, 1998

Figes, Orlando, *A People's Tragedy*, Pimlico, London, 1996

Sema, Robert, *A History of 20th Century Russia*, Penguin, London, 1997

HITLER

Bullock, Alan, *Hitler – A Study in Tyranny*, Penguin, London, 1962

Kershaw, Ian, *Hitler – Profiles in Power*, Longman, London, 1991

Kershaw, Ian, *Hitler – Hubris and Nemesis*, Penguin, London, 2001

Maser, Werner, *Hitler*, Bechtle, Munich, 1971

FRANÇOIS 'PAPA DOC' DUVALIER

Diederich, Bernard & Burt, Al, *Papa Doc: Haiti and its Dictator*,
  The Bodley Head, 1970
Ferguson, James, *Papa Doc, Baby Doc*, Blackwell Publishers, 1988

[1] From *Papa Doc: Haiti and its Dictator* by Bernard Diederich & Al Burt,
  Penguin Books, 1969.
[2] From 'Tyranny and Enlightenment in Haiti and Britain' by David Hawkes,
  published in *Bad Subjects*, Issue 30, February 1997
[3] From *Papa Doc: Haiti and its Dictator* by Bernard Diederich & Al Burt,
  Penguin Books, 1969.
[4] The Mahotières bomb (30 April 1958) was originally put down to Louis
  Dejoie who, in order to escape Duvalier and his thugs, requested asylum in
  the Mexican Embassy. The Pétionville bomb (29 June 1958) was put down
  to an iron-worker called Kelly Thompson who later implicated the Jumelles.
[5] This support was due for the most part to America's long-term obsession
  with anti-communism for they believed that by helping Haiti economically
  the government would not sway to the left as in nearby Cuba.

POL POT

Chandler, David P., *Brother Number One: A Political Biography of Pol Pot*,
  Westview, Oxford, 1999
Jackson, Karl D., *Cambodia 1975-1978 – Rendevouz with Death*,
  Princeton, 1989
Kiernan, Ben, *The Pol Pot Regime*, Yale University Press, 1996
Martin, M. A., *Cambodia – A Shattered Society*, University of
  California Press, 1994

IDI AMIN

Jamison, Martin, *Idi Amin and Uganda: an annotated bibliography*,
Greenwood, London, 1992
Listowel, J. H., *Amin*, IUP Books, Dublin, 1973
Martin, David, *General Amin*, Faber, London, 1974
Mutibwa Phares, *Uganda Since Independence*, Hurst, London, 1992

SADDAM HUSSEIN

Aburish, Säid K., *Saddam Hussein: The Politics of Revenge*, Bloomsbury, London 2001

Rivers Pitt, William, & Ritter, Scott, *War on Iraq*, Profile Books, London 2002

Pilger, John, *Hidden Agendas*, London 1998

www.kuwait-info.org/Gulf_War/amnesty_international.html

[1] Some people doubt this date, believing instead that Saddam was born on 1 July 1939.

[2] Put simply, Iraq is split into two main factions – the Sunni and Shia Muslims. This schism began as far back as AD680 and still accounts for much of the blood that has been shed in Iraq over the centuries.

[3] From *Saddam Hussein The Politics of Revenge* by Säid K. Aburish, published by Bloomsbury publishing plc 2000.

[4] From *Saddam Hussein The Politics of Revenge* by Säid K. Aburish, published by Bloomsbury publishing plc 2000.

[5] Saddam has two sons, Udday and Qussay Hussein, both of whom have followed in their father's footsteps to become men of violence.

[6] www.kuwait-info.org/Gulf_War/amnesty_international.html

OSAMA BIN LADEN

Reeve, Simon, *The New Jackals: Ramzi Yousef, Osama bin Laden and the Future of Terrorism*, London 1999

Marsden, Peter, *The Taliban: War, Religion and the New Order in Afghanistan*, Oxford 1998

[1] Rahimullah Usufzai, 'Conversation with Terror', *Time*, 11 January 1998.

[2] John Simpson, 'The day bin Laden tried to have me killed', *Sunday Telegraph*, 23 August 1998.

[3] In 1994 the Saudi government revoked bin Laden's citizenship, citing his political activities.

[4] Hamid Mir, interview with Osama bin Laden, Pakistan, 18 March 1997.

[5] 'War just started, says bin Laden', Associated Press, 23 August 1998.

[6] Extract from the text of Osama bin Laden's fatwa, published in *Al Quds al-Arabi*, 23 February 1998.

[7] From the text of President Bush's address to the nation, 11 September 2001.

[8] From the *Observer*, 7 October 2001.